THE WHITE ELEPHANT

For Muslimahs looking for practical tips
on marital issues.

BY
AISHAH ADAMS

Bismillaah – In the name of Allaah

Design by www.revoflightdesign.com

CONTENTS

DEDICATION

This book is dedicated to Allaah (subhaanahu wa ta'ala), the only One deserving of worship, the One who created the pen and asked it to write. I dedicate this piece to Him, Al-Waduud. I pray that He, Al-Kareem, accepts this as a means to earning His pleasure and brings honour to me and my family by virtue of this book. Aamiyn.

I also dedicate this to the noblest of mankind, an-Nabiy (sallallaahu alayhi wasallam) for teaching us ways to cope with life's challenges. May Allaah continually send blessings upon him and his household till the end of time.

This piece is also dedicated to my dear parents, my lovely husband and every member of my family for being so awesome and supportive of my dreams and aspirations. You mean the world to me.

Lastly, I dedicate this book to every Muslimah who has been through the rough patches of marriage and/or divorce, and I sincerely hope the next generation will have a better go at it. This is for you all. May you find peace, aamiyn.

ACKNOWLEDGEMENTS

Alhamdulilaahi Rabbil 'alameen

All praise and adoration are due to Allaah (subhaanahu wa ta'ala) by whose leave all righteous deeds are completed. May the peace and blessings of Allaah (subhaanahu wa ta'ala) be upon the noblest of mankind, Muhammad ibn Abdullah (sallAllaahu alayhi wasallam), his household, his companions, and all those who follow his teachings till the Day of Qiyamah.

I bear witness that none has the right to be worshipped except Allaah (subhaanahu wa ta'ala), and the Nabiy (sallAllaahu alayhi wasallam) is His slave and messenger and he (sallAllaahu alayhi wasallam) conveyed the message.

I am indeed grateful to my parents for their care, love,training, encouragement, prayers and support all these years; I appreciate their effort in making a success out of me. I appreciate being directed by them to be strong, confident, intelligent, educated, courageous and spiritually conscious. Words alone cannot express my gratitude for all their hard work over the years. I am forever grateful to them for challenging me to be ever optimistic and selfless regardless of what life threw my way. May Allaah grant them the loftiest place in Jannah. *Jazaakumullaahu khayran!*

I am grateful to my beloved husband for being the wind beneath my wings. Thank you for being the man that you are; the one who constantly strives to be a better person everyday. Thank you for being motivated and self-confident. Thank you for accepting me and supporting my work.

To my dear children, I could never express in words how much you mean to me and how much you have changed my life. Being able to call myself a mother is in and of itself a gift from Allaah that I cherish with the whole of my heart. To my siblings - Femi, Aminat, Mariam and Ibrahim, it has been my extreme pleasure to have grown up alongside you all. We had a different childhood, and we, as most families, have been through our fair share of hard times. But I have watched us all persevere, reach and accomplish, Alhamdulillah. I appreciate your being there for me and holding my hands through the storms that have rocked my boat. I am thankful to my in-laws for their continued support and prayers. I appreciate the help of my cousin, Rafiat Oyenaike and Mrs Ahmed for helping me out and making it easy for me to focus on my writing.

I am also thankful to my esteemed teacher, Abu Naasir, for his faith in my strengths and, most importantly, for his encouragement, advice and guidance. Br. Shamsudeen

Ige, *Jazaakumullaahu khayran* for being so awesome. I also appreciate the support and good counsel I got from Abu Hudhayfah Folarin as well as other esteemed teachers I have learnt from along the way.

I am grateful to LaYinka Sanni, my writing coach. Your help, motivation and support was next to none. *Jazaakumullaahu khayran*. I am also grateful to Reyhana Ismail, Segilola Sunmola, Hend Hegazi, Kelli Law, Kaighla White, Eniola Balogun and of course, Tope Ganiyah Fajingbesi for your constructive criticism of my work as well as your help and support in getting me to the finish line. May Allaah grant you all success in this world and in the hereafter. Aamiyn.

I also appreciate the encouragement of Br. Olaniyi Sanuth, Aisha Mijindadi and Ndako Mijindadi.

I am grateful to my lovely friends Kifaayah Umm Khadeejah, Lamide Arogundade, Yinka Bakare, Lateefah Oyefeso, Aramide Fatoyinbo, Salahdeen Saliu Khadeejah, Salahdeen Omoyele Fatimah, Aisha Mosuro, Aisha Oloyede, Aisha Giwa & family, Annam Mustapha, Zainab Khan and all you wonderful people who stood by me through thick and thin. To my Siddiqah sisters: Maryam Sanuth, Simbiat, Sa'adat, Aisha, Alimah, Ganiyah and the rest of you who have been amazing support for the project – you know yourselves: *Jazaakumullaahu khayran*. To the Olajobis, Kafilat Dada, Halimah Odus, Jibril Okin, AbdHakeem Buhari, Idris Taiwo, Kamar Aliu, Idris Adejumo and everyone else who has contributed to the growth of Siddiqah: *Jazaakumullaahu khayran*.

AUTHOR'S INTRODUCTION

All praise and adoration is due to Allaah (subhaanahu wa ta'ala) who has made marriage halal and made fornication *haram*, as He says:
"And of His signs is that He created for you from yourselves mates that you may find tranquillity in them; and He placed between you affection and mercy. Indeed in that are signs for a people who give thought."[1]

In the above verse, Allaah (subhaanahu wa ta'ala) tells us that marriage has been prescribed for us "… that you may find rest…." If this is one of the reasons for the permissibility of *nikah*, why then is there so much unrest in most of our marriages?

Like every other aspect of our deen, it is important that we study and become well-informed, not only about the right way to proceed when seeking to marry, but also about how to make our marriages work.

This book is a humble effort on my part to assist marriage-seeking Muslims to avoid certain pitfalls, some of which I fell into and were responsible for some trials I eventually had to go through. It is my sincere wish that those seeking to marry will pay attention to my advice in this book and apply reason and caution when searching for a spouse - especially the sisters!

One of my teachers once said to me, "Do you know it is important for a sister to look carefully and be sure of what she is agreeing to when she accepts the *khitbah* (marriage proposal) of a brother? It would be foolhardy of her to accept the *khitbah* of a tyrant." At the time, I thought, 'SubhanAllaah!' Why didn't we sisters think of marriage in this way before we got in?' *Alhamdulilaahi Rabbil 'alameen* for everything.

What makes me qualified to write this book? I have a background in public health. I am also trained in crisis intervention and disaster management as well as in life coaching. I have thus combined the knowledge gathered from these trainings to work in the capacity as a marriage and personal development coach.

Furthermore, my experiences in the 'field' of marriage has equipped me with wisdom and knowledge, some of which I am now sharing through this book. I have seen the good of it, the bad of it, and the very bitter end of it; and I hope to be able to

---

1. Surah ar-Room, 21

assist others from falling into the same ditch I once fell into. What does it profit me to see my sisters in pain? Pain that could have been avoided if they received good counsel before marriage or during the marriage when problems began to spiral out of control? Counselling should be sought not only before marriage, but also during marriage to help prevent its collapse, as wise counsel is not only preventive, but also reactive.

I have also supported those who have had to deal with the harsh hand of failed marriages via my work at Siddiqah, a non-governmental organisation I founded in 2013. I started Siddiqah to support widows, divorcees, and struggling families, to empower other Muslimahs to live productive lives and to render health promotion and education services around specific health issues. I work with other counsellors and therapists to help restore stability to those whose lives have been negatively affected by the loss of a spouse either through death or divorce.

Though the journey so far has been saddled with roadblocks, I am positive things will take shape soon, and in record time, more Muslimahs will be able to get back on their feet through the support and help Allaah gives us permission to provide through the work we do at Siddiqah.

In order to cover marital-related issues to consider before and after marriage, this book is organised in 3 sections. The 'before' section focuses on pre-marital guidance, whilst the 'after' section is about how to navigate through marriage once you step in, as well as how to cope with marital discord that could lead to divorce in the event the marriage ship capsizes.

This book aims to present the topic of marriage in Islam in a practical way such that the reader can visualise the realities of marriage and be well-prepared to face the challenges head-on as opposed to going in and realising marriage is not a fairy tale, as typically assumed. There are lots of books that advise on the rights of the husband and wife - however practical, it is not necessarily easy to implement if one has not done the necessary ground work that will make acting on those pieces of advice plausible.

As to why I chose the name 'The White Elephant' - marital issues are rife in our communities at the moment, with many of them resulting in divorce. There has been an influx of divorce cases lately and a good number of them have children being dragged into the mess. You would think that many would take this as a sign to address the problem, but the opposite is true.

Marital issues are often swept under the rug and many people act like everything is fine when in truth, it isn't. If this silence continues, the next generation might suffer even more from the aftermath of this problem than the present generation. Thus, 'The White Elephant' signifies an obvious problem that isn't being addressed as it ought to.

If the discussion in this book helps even one person stay clear of making lifelong mistakes, then *Alhamdulilaah*, I would have achieved my purpose of writing. Any good found in this book is from Allaah (subhaanahu wa ta'ala), for only He inspires and aids one to benefit His slaves, and any error in this book is mine alone, and I ask Allaah to forgive me and accept this work as a means to seeking His Face and His pleasure.

O, our Lord! Grant us in our mates and offspring the joy of our eyes, and make us guides to those who guard (against evil). Aamiyn!

And in the end, *Alhamdulilaahi Rabbil 'alameen.*

Aishah Adams
Lagos, Nigeria | Sha'ban, 1437 (June, 2016)

SECTION 1:
BEFORE YOU STEP IN

The Prophet (sallAllaahu alayhi wasallam) said, "The religion is naseehah (sincerity)." We said, "To whom?" He (sallAllaahu alayhi wasallam) said, "To Allaah, His Book, His Messenger, and to the leaders of the Muslims and their common folk." - *Muslim*

"Being single is not a disease." - *Aisha Giwa*

CHAPTER 1
THINK CAREFULLY AND DO
ADEQUATE RESEARCH

If you were to go on a vacation, you would make adequate preparations to ensure your trip goes smoothly. It wouldn't be presumptuous to assume you would pack your bags to ensure you have enough clothes and toiletries to guarantee some level of comfort, and you would confirm your flight is correctly booked for your intended destination. It would seem impossible for you to book a flight to Gabon when in fact you are headed to Egypt. You would do your research before departure so you wouldn't just wing it and go with the flow.

In the same way, you have to be prepared when you intend to marry. Your journey is much smoother when you have some background information about the intended destination. All journeys have their twists and turns. Sometimes we hit a dead-end and at such times, we are forced to take a few steps back to re-align. Likewise, marriage is an odyssey two people embark on, consistently travelling with similar goals in mind.

Sometimes, I think to myself, 'Why do we invest so much on a journey of a few days or months or years, yet barely invest enough time and research in a journey we intend to embark on for a lifetime?' An expedition more important and noteworthy to prepare extensively for is this journey where you are a key player: Marriage. This journey isn't always smooth; sometimes the path leads towards happiness and sometimes towards misery. The level of preparation for this journey matters as it has a direct impact, not only on our lives, but on the lives of those around us.

When I set out to embark on this voyage at an early stage of my life, I didn't fully comprehend the concept of marriage. And alas! My lack of preparation led to catastrophic consequences I have had to live with and learn from. Just like you do not get the opportunity to re-live a particular journey from the beginning, the same goes for marriage. If you are fortunate, you get to retrace some steps, but only a small percentage of married women are able to achieve this feat. However commendable, they still don't get to begin the journey on the once-clean slate they had at the very start of their marriage. Just as a stamped passport signifies your new status as a traveller enabling you to bid farewell to your home, a sealed marriage contract signifies your new status as a wife, enabling you to bid farewell to singledom. In the event of the marriage hitting a rock and capsizing either intentionally or otherwise, you either become widowed, divorced, or separated.

Marriage is a sacred institution and is from the signs of Allaah (subhaanahu wa ta'ala) as He says:

"And of His signs is that He created you from dust; then, suddenly you were human beings dispersing [throughout the earth]."[2]

It is from His signs and it is important that you cohabit in love and mercy with the person you choose to spend the rest of your life with as explained by this verse. At this point, you'd probably wonder why do we then have so much rancour going on in our marriages today? Why has there been an increase in rates of divorce in our communities today? While it could be a consequence of our straying away from purpose-filled unions, I believe it goes back to a lack of adequate preparation for the journey ahead, which then results in avoidable turbulence, which sometimes leads us to call it quits instead of retracing our steps to continue the journey on a stronger footing.

I wish I had focused more on the psychological preparation required for marriage, as well as cross-checked the itinerary for my life goals to ensure it coincided with that of the spouse I was intending to accept as my *qawwam* (leader). At the time, I believed the most important questions to ask were those that lay emphasis on how much Qur'an a person had memorised and how much attachment to the deen a person had. I was not interested in dragging out the courtship period as I had come across a piece that described the *nikah* of Ali (radiyAllaahu anhu) to Faatimah (radiyAllaahu anha).

The article explained how Ali (radiyAllaahu anhu) went straight to meet the Nabiy of Allaah (sallAllaahu alayhi wasallam) when he intended marriage to Faatimah (radiyAllaahu anha). It further explained that Faatimah (radiyAllaahu anha) didn't speak to Ali (radiyAllaahu anhu) despite being related to him! She only initiated discussions with him after her father (sallAllaahu alayhi wasallam) consented to the union. For me, this showed Faatimah's deep sense of trust in Allaah as well as in the responsibility Allaah (subhaanahu wa ta'ala) had placed in the hands of her guardian.

2. Surah ar-Room: 20

She was patient and eventually enjoyed the dividends of her patience as it translated into goodness for her in the marriage.

Upon reading this, I silently vowed to strive to emulate this practice, so I kept my questions brief and didn't dig as deeply as I should have. Perhaps a better approach would have been to let the proposals come to me through my father as was the case with Faatimah (radiyAllaahu anha). I believed that if a person strove to obey Allaah and had an attachment to the deen of Allaah, all else would be added on to them.

Yes, this is the ideal but we are not living in those times anymore; sadly, we are more theoretical than practical when it comes to the deen and my naivety at the time eventually cost me a lot. I wish I had researched into the family I was marrying into, I wish I had asked more people about him at the time… I wish… I wish… I wish. Alhamdulilah in all circumstances.

Now, that was my mistake, my error, my story. You can avoid falling into the wrong boat I fell in if you do adequate research before you agree to spend the rest of your life in this world and in the *akhirah* with someone, as marriage in Islam does not end in the life of this world; it continues in the next life for the righteous ones.

WHAT DO YOU WANT?

If you were to ask a group of young couples why they got married, my guess is 80% of them only did so to fulfil their growing sexual curiosity without committing *zina*; while for some, it was merely due to societal pressure as we all know there is a silent stigma attached to a woman once she hits a certain age. Would you say these reasons are good enough reasons to embark on a journey that 'ends' only in the hereafter? No, I don't think so.

Many go into marriage with no clue as to why they are getting married and with no idea how to paddle the boat. This cluelessness has led to an increase in divorce rates - almost to epidemic proportions - thus, there is a need to address this issue before it completely devours the fragment of civility left amongst a number of Muslim families.

One of the first steps to take when seeking a spouse is to ensure you know exactly what your own values are and, more importantly, to define what your life goals are. If you don't know yourself and you have no clue as to what you want out of life, the tendency of you falling into the wrong hands is high. Why? Because you will probably go along with the first person that hints at marriage, having the basic characteristics you think you seek. Imagine if you then discover yourself a few years down the line and you start to act differently; it leads to lots of friction and the beginning of trouble. Please know what you are getting yourself into before you say 'yes'! This is paramount because the moment you accept the proposal and the marriage contract is sealed, everything changes for you. If there is anything I want you to take from this section of the book it is this: Think carefully about what you are about to do before you do it.

PURIFY AND CLARIFY YOUR INTENTIONS

Umar ibn al-Khattab narrated that the Prophet (sallAllaahu alayhi wasallam) said, "The reward of deeds depends upon the intentions, and every person will get the reward according to what he has intended. So whoever emigrated for worldly benefits or for a woman to marry, his emigration was for what he emigrated for." [3]

This hadith helps us understand the great importance placed on our intention for every action or decision we decide to embark upon. Thus, it is important that you are clear on why you are getting married, as this clarity will not only go a long way in shaping your thoughts and reactions when the reality of marriage finally sets in, but it will determine what you get out of it.

Now, marriage can be really beautiful when you go on the journey with the right person and it can be really depressing - amongst other things - if you let yourself begin the journey uninformed and clueless, as is often the case in a number of Muslim marriages I've been privileged to know about.

Please, ensure you are clear on *why* you are getting married just as much as *who* you intend to marry. Do not get entangled in marriage with the 'wrong' person just because you were too shy to speak up when you should have, or you were worried about presenting a wrong image of yourself. Realise that people will judge you irrespective of what you do, so how about you make this marriage decision one that you really want and where you would be happy to be patient through its struggles? Do not allow **anybody** to push you into making a marital choice or decision that you are not ready to stick up for when the going gets tough.

I remember when I was going to get married the first time: I had only known him for a little over a month, and because *eeman* was glowing in my heart, I was very strict about no courtship. I made my parents understand this as well and they went along with me, so the solemnisation of the marriage was conducted in no time. I hadn't

---

3. Sahih al-Bukhari

moved in with him or formally announced it, so I sort of still had the opportunity to bail-out.

A few weeks before the walimah, I started getting worried as I'd been talking to him freely and had come to realise we were a perfect mismatch. Our wedding feast was meant to mark the day I would officially move in with him and we'd announce the marriage. Rather than feeling elated, I was worried I'd cause my parents a lot of embarrassment since they had started sending out invites for the *nikah*. I hid these feelings and didn't say anything. I came to regret my silence as the marriage headed for the rocks from the beginning. We had barely lived together for one and a half months when it became clear to me I had made the biggest mistake ever! Knowing what I know now, it was key for me to get my intentions in order before agreeing to marrying anyone. *QadarAllaahu wa maa shaa af'ala.*

AN ASIDE: ADVICE TO PARENTS
Dear Parents,

Please, please, and please do not give in to that feeling nagging at you to mount pressure on your children to get married, or to compare them with others with statements such as: "O, Khadeejah, don't you have someone? Oh, I saw Lateefah today and she's getting ready for her wedding." Or, "O, Saeedah is already pregnant with her 2nd child and you are yet to get married." These, and many other such statements, are the reason why a number of young people fail to take their time when committing to *nikah*. You can't expect them not to jump into the arms of the first person they see when you place such pressure on them.

Furthermore, it is important that we make the home a safe and enjoyable haven for our children; a place wherein they look forward to spending time, and not somewhere from which they wish to run away. There are a good number of people - myself included - who have made wrong choices due to the perceived pressure at home - lack of freedom to worship their Rabb as much as they would love to, the constant reminder that peers were getting married and a deficiency on the part of the parent(s) to show love to their children as they ought to.

Please, do **not** push your wards into marriages they are not really interested in. It is important that you maintain a balance - you are *not* a weakling when you take sincere counsel from your children. Though you are older, wisdom is not measured in the number of years on Earth as this is a gift from Allaah (subhaanahu wa ta'ala) and

He blesses whom He wills with it.

I remember when I was young, green-eyed, and looking to get married. I originally wanted to do so for His sake, especially after I came across a hadith that advised parents to let their child go when a person with sound character and religion comes to seek her hand. Somewhere along the line, though, my hurry to be out of my father's house made me jump into marriage with the first person who appeared to be of good character, without looking carefully. In the end, I had no one to blame except myself and it is still one of my deepest regrets. Why do I share this bit of my story with you? So that you will understand that my advice to you is from an avoidable bitter experience.

NO PROMISED SECOND-CHANCES

My dear sister, please realise that not everyone has the opportunity at a 'second chance' - there is no guarantee of this happening, so please heed wise counsel whilst the opportunity to do so still presents itself. You are better off not wallowing in self-pity, as the trauma that accompanies a failed marriage is hard to bear except if Allaah grants ease. Not many are able to pick themselves up after they suffer from the aftermath of a choice gone wrong.

Please do not leave any stone unturned in your quest to find out about your intended spouse. Adequately research who you want to agree to marry before the mantle moves from your hands to his. It is important you ask about the deen and character of your intended spouse from people who have lived with him, travelled with him, and even done business with him before you accept - especially since there is no such thing as courtship in Islam in the way it is now being practised in our society. There is a popular narration of Umar ibn Al-Khattab (radiyAllaahu anhu) in which he asked about the character of a certain man and one of his companions praised him. Then he asked if the man had travelled with him, slept in close proximity with him for a period of 3 days, or had made business transactions with him. Why? Because it is impossible to hide one's true nature for that long.

Umar ibn Al-Khattab (radiyAllaahu anhu) was reported to have said, "Do not be fooled by one who recites the Qur'an. His recitation is but speech - but look to those who act according to it."[4]

Anyone can speak about piety and sound righteous, but only the sincere and truthful

---

4. Al-Khatib, Iqtida' Al-'Ilm Al-'Amal no. 109

ones act on that which they say or at least attempt to act on it.

You can uphold the dictates of Islam by not courting and still act cautiously by seeking information about the personality and character of your intended. Speak to as many people as you can about him; do not get carried away with his outward appearance as looks can be deceptive. Ask close business associates and close friends or family members easily accessible to you. If you are too shy to do this yourself, have a trusted person do these checks on your behalf and make sure you do not discard any information you get because the one you discard may end up being the most vital piece of information ever!

The Yoruba - a native tribe from the south-western region of Nigeria - usually call such appointed detectives, *alarena*. In the days of our parents, the wife's family would always send a trusted but neutral person to find out information about the intended's family, and this *alarena* would feed back their findings to the parents of the bride before allowing them to decide whether or not the family of the intended was worthy of their daughter.

Let me share a short story with you. There was a certain Muslimah looking to get married who learnt from someone that her prospective spouse might have certain health challenges he hadn't disclosed; she assumed the one who gave her the information was just trying to discredit her prospective spouse because he wanted her to marry someone else. She ended up marrying her intended only to find out about 3 years into the marriage that the one who spoke to her about the health challenges of her then prospective spouse was right after all.

There is a lot of stigmatisation of various classes of people, such as those who have been married or those with mental health challenges. This sometimes makes people with these trials hide the truth about themselves. However, this is not a justification for their actions, for if they truly put their trust in Allaah (subhaanahu wa ta'ala), they would understand that the provision and allotment of every human has been decreed and nothing that was meant for them would slip their hands. Nevertheless, the truth still remains that you need to find out as much about them as you can prior to making your final decision.

RESEARCH THE IN-LAWS

Researching the family you are marrying into is vital because when you marry a person, you marry their family as well. There is a popular adage in my native language that says, 'Marrying a bad husband can be tolerable, but having bad in-laws is the worst possession you could have'. There are many instances where the spouse really wants to be amazing, but familial influences make them act otherwise.

The more aligned your familial values are with that of your prospective spouse, the less likely it is that you'll have big issues after marriage. Imagine you marry an extremely ambitious man who is happy to have a wife who is equally productive, yet his family feels a woman ought to dance to her husband's dreams and have none of hers. In the event that you are purpose-driven, you may feel pressured to kill that spirit as it contradicts their idea of who a wife should be. It would be asking for trouble if you announce your ambitious moves in their presence.

Researching the family one is marrying into cannot be overstressed, and one area we often overlook is the traditions and expectations surrounding celebrations and joyous occasions, as they attract a lot of familial involvement. In order to avoid tension, it is a good idea to ask the following questions prior to marriage: What is their opinion about the role of a wife/husband in the home? How do they expect the wife to be with her spouse? What are the compulsory duties they expect her to uphold with them? What are their dos and don'ts?

Make sure you also study your prospective new family in terms of their ideas about child-rearing as it is often an area of dispute in a number of marriages. Do your groundwork well and don't leave anything to chance. Trust me, it is more important and easier on you if you look carefully before accepting the *khitbah* than struggling to find a way to patch a boat that is on the verge of capsizing. Be wise.

TALK ABOUT EVERYTHING UNDER THE SUN

Make sure you discuss everything with your spouse before you step in. Marriage is a contract that has terms and conditions, be sure you understand the rules of the game before you go ahead to sign that contract. The Prophet (sallAllaahu alayhi wasallam) said:

"The condition which most deserves to be fulfilled is that by means of which intimacy is permissible for you." [5]

This hadith helps us understand the great importance and significance of marriage in Islam. It also sets the stage for you to be clear on what you are doing before you commit. Discuss everything with your prospective spouse and do not consider any topic to be insignificant. For instance, a topic you could speak about is money: Would you be allowed to earn money? Is the money earned by either party supposed to be split 50/50? Are you both going to operate a joint account? What amount are you expected to spend on the monthly upkeep of the house? Would you be given personal pocket money? What is the extent of his providing for you? Or is it unlimited?

Peel back the layers and make sure you get down to the root. Apply this across all subjects, such as housing, family, sex, health status, obedience and respect, and - more importantly - communication. As you go along in your discussions, identify your character types and study emotional intelligence extensively; this should help you manage each other more effectively.

Ensure that each person is clear on what to expect if and when the contract is eventually sealed and you both start living together in order to avoid unpleasant surprises along the way. When we want to embark on a career path, we usually study the prerequisites thoroughly. Isn't it more important that marriage is given more extensive study than our careers, since the success or failure of our marriages could either make or mar our career?

LIVING WITH IN-LAWS
When you discuss housing, try to find a way around not living in the same quarters as your in-laws. I advise that you minimise interactions with them in this 'getting-to-know-you' phase as third party interactions tend to complicate things for many young couples. There are a good number of marriages that could have been saved if the couples had lived by themselves.

I personally had a bad experience cohabiting with my in-laws, which also contributed to my marriage's eventual collapse. Whilst I admire the women who are able to live happily with their in-laws, I would not advise a new couple do the same, especially because I feel that every marriage needs its own identity away from prying eyes and constant scrutiny - however harmless - of extended family.

In my naivety at the time, living with my then in-laws was a mistake I wish I hadn't made. I didn't understand the politics involved in being a 'good wife'. For some reason I often felt victimised. I had no privacy, and was often called-out for trying to turn their son against them in the event that we decide to make our own traditions, such as visiting my family the day after 'Eid, or having a dinner date without the extended family.

There were days I would sit in the living room of our apartment and just cry my eyes out. It was almost like we were being monitored and my then in-laws were trying to ensure that my ex and I wouldn't become in sync. From my own experience and lots of other stories I have heard, I strongly advise that the couple start out together by living away from outside influences as it allows you and your spouse to get to know each other better, away from the spotlight.

LET'S TALK ABOUT SEX

Marital intimacy is a key topic people shy away from talking about whenever discussing marriage, yet it is an important area of discussion needed closer to the wedding and after marriage so you are well-equipped.

Sex is between 50-90% of a couple's marital life. As such, when there are issues in the sex department, a lot of other aspects of the marriage tend to be affected. There is a need to learn about it because nobody is born with the encyclopaedia of sex activities. We all have to learn different topics at different times, just as we do for other aspects of our life.

I encourage you to read about sexual intimacy and speak to your prospective spouse about it to ascertain his knowledge on the topic. In the event that he has little knowledge, encourage him to learn about it, too. Don't get me wrong, I don't mean he should watch pornography. Porn actually messes up the reality of sex with your spouse as it makes one have unrealistic expectations. By learning, I mean speaking to professionals or marriage counsellors/coaches or reading a number of well-written books on the topic.

Many people go into marriage being clueless about the how, the when, and the why of intimacy. How many people are familiar with the languages of love or with the knowledge of the fact that virgins tend to feel pain at the onset of intimacy? Research this topic and exchange notes with your spouse so that you are both on the same page.

Sadly, I had to suffer at the hands of one who was clueless and who wasn't ready to speak to people or learn about the topic. Whilst I was reading about it and trying to not appear clueless, I neither spoke to him about it nor encouraged him to research the topic. To make matters worse, rather than speak up when things were getting to a head, my decision to keep mute and suck it all in only resulted in a volcanic eruption.

From my own experiences, I believe it is important you ask for everything you possibly need to make the relationship thrive before you make a step towards living together. People tend to work harder and smarter when there is something at stake or when they want to speed up a process.

After all due protocols have been observed, make lots of du'a for guidance from Allaah (subhaanahu wa ta'ala) and stay within the confines of the deen even when you do so. Put your trust in Allaah and have certainty that you have sought help from the best of those who guide as He (subhaanahu wa ta'ala) says:
*"And (we) will provide for him from where he does not expect. **And whoever relies upon Allaah - then He is sufficient for him. Indeed, Allaah will accomplish His purpose.** Allaah has already set for everything a [decreed] extent"* [6]

My du'a for those looking to marry:
May Allaah (subhaanahu wa ta'ala) guide you as you carefully research your prospective spouse; May He guide you to making the best decision that translates to goodness and tranquillity in marriage as well as goodness in the akhirah. Aamiyn.

POINTS TO PONDER:
Adequately research your prospective spouse by asking about him from both friends and foes and business associates and old acquaintances. Ensure you do not disregard any information you gather so that your decision to either accept or decline is based on facts.

Do not limit your research to the prospective spouse alone. Also find out about the family you are marrying into.

Ensure your life goals and dreams complement one another and are not worlds apart.

Please do not ignore any red flags you notice before the wedding - be ready to live with your spouse expecting no change from him - that way, in the event he doesn't change positively, you don't become overly angered.

Please do not go into marriage having high expectations. The huge disappointment that follows such high expectations is often a ship wrecker.

Discuss every topic under the sun with your prospective spouse, from money matters

---

6. Surah at-Talaq: 3

to sex to family to communication. Leave no stone unturned.

Make lots of du'a and put your trust in Allaah.

Remember: You are the architect of your own fortune or misfortune in marriage, so be wise and take good counsel.

CHAPTER 2
ENSURE YOU HAVE MATCHING GOALS

Have you ever thought what it would feel like to be stuck in an alien body? This is what having mismatched goals with your intended feels like to me.

So when you decide to settle down, ensure you marry someone who shares similar dreams and aspirations as you, not the opposite. Believe me when I say, opposites do NOT attract where life goals are concerned. Settling for someone who has an entirely different mindset about achieving success is akin to setting yourself up for marital agony, leading to you feeling embittered and heartbroken if he eventually puts a log in your wheels as you strive to progress.

It might be something as little as you not wanting to live in a certain city and him insisting he lives there because that's where his support system is. Know that marriage is not supposed to be about one person, so get a clear picture of his life goals and how he hopes to go about achieving them. For instance, does he even have clearly set goals or is he just painting a broken chair just to make it look attractive?

What does he think his spouse should have in terms of achievement? It's really important you know all of this.

Some people want to marry a well-educated woman just so they can show off to their friends - the more educated she is the better. Then after they have her living with them, they start to hand out rules that make one wonder why they married her in the first place. If they knew they weren't interested in her improving herself after marriage, why didn't they state that clearly at the onset of their meeting? Why wait until she has settled into a routine with them? It is so frustrating for you as the woman because you just feel like you have just shot yourself in the foot by going along with such an arrangement. Then you start to think, and in some cases say, "I wish I knew this was what he wanted from me", "I wish I had asked him this", "I wish I had asked him about that." Don't wish, act now while you still can. No one ever took ill from answering questions - not that I know of.

His idea of success should tally with your idea of success so that the friction would not be too much. My life goals are numerous; some call me ambitious, but I believe the people of Jannah are purpose-driven who don't see anything as an obstacle. SubhanAllaah, sometimes I think to myself, 'Do I want to enter the same Jannah as these people, yet do so little?' I guess that very thought shaped my life goals, so I wanted to do this and that and I had a number of ways I hoped to achieve the dream of leaving my footprints in the sands of time.

Being a determined and proactive person means I dive right in when I am looking to achieve something, but that probably came across as me trying to take the reins and be in charge. May Allaah forgive us all our shortcomings. Perhaps there were more subtle ways to show I was purpose-driven; but at the time I didn't understand why I had to dampen my sparkle just so my ex could shine. I don't think his lack of zeal to push ahead surfaced only after marriage. I feel he was always that way, I just misread the signs as him being quiet. I turned a blind eye to the blaring warning signs and later wished I hadn't. I gave excuses for all the red flags whenever anyone brought them up.

I didn't ask the right questions and even when certain events came up, I didn't question them well enough, even though I had the opportunity to do so at the time. Perhaps it was partly because I didn't understand the importance of looking carefully; I just told myself there was no need to dig deep since I had put my trust in Allaah. This is an error made by a number of young people zealous about the deen - it's beautiful to trust Allaah, but guess what? It's even better when you work hard and put your trust in Allaah. In fact, in order to complete all the steps of *istikharah*[7], seeking wise counsel is one of the hurdles to jump.

Here are some suggestion of goal-related topics to discuss with a prospective spouse before you accept a proposal:

HEALTH
What are your health goals? What is your intended's health goals? Should one have health goals? Perhaps. What is important, though, is that whatever you want for your health in terms of goodness should tally with the health goals your partner-to-be wants as well. Imagine if, for example, you wanted to keep your slim figure and shape because an increased weight on your part predisposes you to certain health issues due to some inherited health traits, but your to-be's ideal spouse is someone

7. A prayer for guidance when one wants to make a decision about a matter

chubby and really fleshy. He may desire this because his culture associates positive connotations to thickset women. Going ahead with a union of this kind might be asking for trouble.

If, on the flip side, you are super chubby - perhaps due to familial traits - and you seem to be working hard at dropping some pounds, but almost nothing works; then you land yourself with an intended spouse whose idea of the 'perfect' wife is a really slim woman; entering into such an arrangement may not be the best idea.

Again, imagine you aren't a vegetarian and you decide to go ahead with someone who doesn't understand why anyone should have meat in their meals and would usually go to lengths to ensure people around them went with this flow. Do you think a union of this kind would work? You see a lot of the time, these sorts of people have squabbles based on something as trivial as the kind of meal they had or the way you have to look; when the pressure gets too much, it can lead to the collapse of the union.

If you have reservations about certain health goals your intended has, yet you go ahead with the union, failure to uphold that particular health goal is tantamount to disobeying Allaah (subhaanahu wa ta'ala) as obedience to the husband when he doesn't call you to something displeasing to Allaah (subhaanahu wa ta'ala) is an act of worship.

Ibn Hibbaan narrated that Abu Hurayrah (radiyAllaahu anhu) said: The Prophet (sallAllaahu alayhi wasallam) said: "If a woman prays her five (daily prayers), fasts her month (Ramadhan), guards her chastity and **obeys her husband**, it will be said to her: 'Enter Paradise from whichever of the gates of Paradise you wish.'"[8]

You might think this issue is trivial, but trust me when I say some marriages have been known to break down based on things even more minor than health goals!

WEALTH

It is common practice in a number of cultures for some people to have issues with their spouse concerning wealth and wealth creation.

Finance is one of the biggest causes of divorce in a number of communities, hence

---

8. Classed as sahih by Shaykh al-Albaani in Sahih al-Jaami', no. 660

the need to discuss wealth creation with your spouse to-be. What is their idea of what a wife should do in terms of wealth creation?

Please do not assume that since he's educated, he will want you to pursue a career and have some sort of financial stability. I have come to notice that although some men love to see their sisters as well as other female relatives make progress in their careers, they do not seem to want the same for their wives. They hide under the cover that their 'love' for her makes it hard for them to see her go through stress - this is for those who even care to state this nicely. Others say she'd 'grow wings' if allowed to have financial freedom and wealth creation avenues, thus, put obstacles in the way towards her wealth creation goals.

On the flip side there are some women who, in my opinion, go overboard in their bid to 'stay at home and not display themselves like times of ignorance'. Their understanding of not displaying themselves is limited to the point that engaging in financially rewarding and productive ventures from home is a problem for them as well. This makes it equally hard for a man whose idea of the ideal wife is someone who can stand on her two feet, not necessarily because he wants her to contribute to the day-to-day running of the home, but because he loves the idea of an independent woman regardless of whether he is around or not. If we read through the *seerah* of the Nabiy (sallAllaahu alayhi wasallam), we would read about the contributions of a number of women to Islam, both in wealth and strength. Wanting one's wife to be gainfully employed is thus not far from the ideal, BUT it has to agree with her goals for wealth.

It is important to strike a balance between your wealth goals and that of your to-be spouse in order to avoid grounds for unnecessary squabbles and heartache.

RELATIONSHIPS

What kind of relationship do you want to maintain with your parents after marriage? How do you want to relate with your in-laws? How about your siblings and their spouses? Your friends? How are you expected to socialise? All these questions need to be clarified before you go into a marriage.

I had barely been married for two weeks when my husband at the time said to me, "I thought women don't go back to see their families after they marry, according to our cultural values," and I thought, "Oh! Now you remember we have cultural values, right! How come you forgot all about the culture before we got married?" Being from a royal family, he could have spent an arm and a leg in order to pay for the cultural marriage rites. It was convenient not to embrace cultural rites before we got married, but suddenly cultural practices played a role in the marriage.

Again, this experience of mine made me realise how poorly prepared I was when I ventured near the institute of marriage during the early part of my life and I hope you won't make similar mistakes. Be clear on what your relationships - especially with your family - will be like and how you'd like them to evolve after marriage. If you have differing views on it, it's better you don't go ahead expecting him to change and eventually 'fall in love' with your family because in the event he doesn't budge after marriage, you might be falling into a big trial of severing kinship ties. May Allaah save you from such. Aamiyn.

EDUCATION

I had a number of educational goals before I got married, such as studying till the PhD level at the minimum and getting a second degree in a different discipline (Islamic studies and/or Psychology), just to mention a couple of examples. I made sure I discussed them with my ex before we got married and he seemed to go along with it. Little did I know this 'support' of the idea of me studying was just a smoke screen to cover who he really was. I was so excited at the prospect of doing my master's degree with my husband, I immediately began researching schools and ways to fund our fees, ensuring I carried him along with every step. He wasn't really interested in studying, though. He was able to mask his lack of enthusiasm and subtly hinted at learning a skill instead. I thought it was because he didn't realise there were other avenues to improve his knowledge base. *What a joke! I thought I married an engineer not a mechanic.* I thought I was showing him other ways and I became adamant, but this only caused us to drift apart further and made our differences even more crystal clear. In the end, I wished I could take back all I ever did to make our educational goals match as it only caused more problems. I should have walked away **before** marriage. *Alhamdulilaah 'alaa kulli haal.*

If you are purpose-driven with a clear vision of what you want for yourself, do not settle for someone who has no sense of direction and just goes with the wind. Make sure you are both clear on how far you intend to go in your educational career. As a wife and possible mother, you'll need a lot of support from your husband, just as much as he needs your understanding and support through his life goals as well. In the event you are both on different wavelengths with respect to how much more you can study after marriage, don't assume he'll change his mind after marriage; understand that agreeing to this means a forfeit of your initial goals in the event you both marry. You can't marry him knowing he had certain ideas about you studying more, and then start to tear out your hair when your greatest fears come to light. Please ask pertinent questions, be sure you are satisfied with how much or little he wants you to achieve, so it doesn't pose a threat to your marriage if you eventually go ahead.

SPIRITUALITY

What's your level of spirituality? Are you content where you are, or are you prepared to invest time and effort in your spiritual growth? What role would you want your spouse to play in your spiritual growth? What is the *aqeedah* of your partner-to-be? Do you both follow the same methodology? Who are your teachers? Who are his teachers?

There are loads of questions you can ask, as spirituality is another major cause of discord amongst couples. Sometimes, a couple start out being on the same level of spirituality, sometimes they're on varying levels. Nevertheless, having spiritual goals that are too vast can be a source of contention. While both men and women dedicated to the worship of Allaah love to be married to someone who helps them with growth in their *eeman*, sadly there are times when we use the wrong yardstick to measure a spouse-to-be's level of spirituality. The length or thickness of a brother's beard is not a measure of how spiritually-conscious he is; neither does the shortness of his trousers say anything! The fact that he has memorised the entire Qur'an as well as *Sahih al-Bukhari* still doesn't reinforce any point. What does reflect his spirituality is his manners. Study his manners carefully and, more importantly, ask around.

How do his manners correlate with the knowledge he gathers about the deen? Does he act on knowledge, or does he only use it in arguments against Muslims who he perceives to have a lower understanding than him? Please don't let appearance or the friends he moves around with influence your decisions, as he could be the black sheep amongst the white flock. Of course, the opposite could also be true, but be sure to gather your information about him.

CAREER

What are your career goals? Have you factored in family? What are your plans for this as well? If you know you'd rather have a career in something that gives you freedom with your time, don't go accepting the proposal of someone who clearly wants his wife to work full-time, even though he knows they aren't in your career goals.

I remember explaining to my ex that my idea of success was making money from the corner of my room in order to have time for my family. At the time, he acted like it was really a good idea; in the end, after the seeds of discord had been sown, he started saying to everyone that cared to listen that he didn't think it made sense that I didn't go out looking for a job even though I had clearly told him my idea of success!

There is no point trying to force your ideals on an unwilling partner, so please, be kind enough to yourself and stay clear of a person whose ideals are worlds apart from yours.

Whatever you do, please try to talk about these topics presented above and ensure you both have a similar understanding on each one of these areas as it helps create a stronger bond between the couple in the long run. The more similar a couple are, the better and easier the bonding process. Although it is impossible to have a smooth ride without friction now and then - especially during the early stages of a new relationship - it is possible to have a relatively peaceful and loving connection if one's values correspond with that of the spouse-to-be. And Allaah knows best.

POINTS TO PONDER:

Discuss extensively your goals for health, wealth, education, spirituality, relationships and career choices.

Try to document your conversations and review your discussions now and then.

Take your wali along - this helps him advise on whether to go ahead with the *nikah* or not.

The Pen is lifted and the ink has dried; when we have striven hard in our bid to tie the camel, whatever happens after that is good in and of itself.

CHAPTER 3
DO **NOT** COMPROMISE OR LOWER YOUR STANDARDS

Ibn Qayyim said, "If a person is sincere towards Allaah in all his affairs, Allaah will give him more than He gives to others, and this sincerity results from true love of Allaah and true trust in Him. So the sincerest of people is the one who loves Allaah most and puts most trust in Him."[9]

There is a certain level of confidence that comes with complete reliance on Allaah (subhaanahu wa ta'ala) that none has except the *mutawwakilun* - those who have unshakeable trust in Allaah, no matter what comes their way. This certainty is followed by an assurance that the sky is the stepping stone for one's dreams. This, my dear, is how I would love for you to live your life, especially when the time comes for you to choose a lifelong partner and settle down. Be sincere in your intentions to settle down, and just like Ibn Qayyim (rahimahullaah) said, Allaah will give you better than you ever hoped for, In Shaa Allaah.

I, like many young people whom Allaah blessed with the ability to be focused, had dreams and aspirations in my younger years. I had a long list of dreams I hoped to realise: married by 25, with at least 3 toddlers by 30; a budding career and a loving husband to snuggle with at night. Getting divorced was definitely not part of my grand scheme. My dreams were almost shattered when I took a key step in the wrong direction: I chose to accept the proposal of one whose lifelong dreams did not align with mine. I chose to saddle myself with one who was ready to settle for mediocrity - a direct opposite of the values my parents instilled in me.

In my attempt to salvage the ship from capsizing, I almost lost myself and my identity in its entirety. Alhamdulilah for the blessing of waking up from my slumber and retracing my steps. Unfortunately, my reawakening was inconsequential to the poor decisions I had previously made. Attempting to save the ship - my marriage - at that time was like embarking on a preposterous exercise. SubhanAllaah, I did all I could, but truly, Allaah does what He wills. I am strong-willed - I know this - but in my

---

9. Al-Fawaaid, p136-187

attempt to hold on to my dreams, I came across as being too assertive.

Sometimes in life, we try to wake an obviously dead horse when it would have been wiser to expend energy to ensure it's doing well, thus preventing the catastrophic end of a horse that was once seen as lovely. This is the similitude of what happens in some marriages.

At the time of the proposal, it was apparent that I was accepting to be with someone I wasn't in love with; we didn't flow and the connection wasn't as I had envisaged. We neither had the physical nor emotional connection I had anticipated - at least at my end, though he appeared quite taken by me.

My ex had a demure outlook; very studious and religious - these were the traits I thought mattered. I didn't mind that we barely had things to say whenever we met. I assumed he was shy because we always had my *mahram* lurking in the corner to ensure we didn't commit fornication. He kept lowering his gaze and this made me think, 'Maa Shaa Allaah - *nice!'* The thought that a man in our environment and times would not even look me in the eye directly made me think highly of his deen. 'He certainly would make a fine husband', I thought.

I was thoroughly disappointed once we got married. The chemistry was still amiss and we still had nothing to say even when we were in the confines of our small room. Sex was a chore as we were both inexperienced and he wasn't willing to explore, learn, or even speak to professionals. I guess his ego was in the way. I would just lie there sometimes, listening to his heavy breathing while hoping it would end soon.

I wasn't exactly looking to have butterflies in my tummy, but neither was I expecting to have no emotional connection whatsoever. I went along because of that popular saying that 'opposites attract'. Little did I know that this was limited to physics and that in the real world of relationships, the more the similarities between a couple, the more likely their relationship was going to work.

I was in my final year of university and was ready to explode with all the ideas I had. I was expecting a support system in my husband, but I quickly realised that my ideals were not his and vice-versa. I was far too independent for my own good, as he had expected me to make the home my only priority; on the flip side, he was quite dependent on his family to make his decisions and that was a harsh reality to deal with. I thought perhaps I could change his views, make him a manly-man who supports his wife's goals and cheers on her dreams. That mistake is something I am still paying for. With what I know now, I realise it was a true test of my faith. I, who boasted to myself that I trusted in Allaah, faltered miserably when it was time to act on my belief. The weakness of my faith is what cost me a lot more than I realised I would suffer.

Tawakkul in Allaah (subhaanahu wa ta'ala) is usually accompanied with *sabr* - patience. You should trust that when the time is right and when it is best for you, the right person will come along. It's okay to be determined, but ensure your determination isn't such that will lead you to forcing yourself into situations waiting to go bad. *Alhamdulilaah* for my life lessons.

Why do I share this with you? Because I don't want you to re-live my life experience. I believe you can have a happy-ever-after with your spouse if you invest in the right person. It is my hope that when you decide to accept a proposal, it would be from one whose ideals match yours. I pray you won't get overly emotional like I did, and subject yourself to ridicule afterwards. My sister once said to me,"If you marry someone out of pity, know that he will not pity you when roles change. He is more likely to treat you with impunity."This has been the case for a number of marriages I've come across in recent times, mine included, even though I didn't realise that at the time. Do not accept a proposal hoping that the person will change to what you consider ideal. If he is not at the level you want him, it's important not to settle for anything less than what you feel you deserve, because a failed marriage hurts your pride and self-worth.

DON'T IMAGINE YOU CAN CHANGE HIM

Couples often get married hoping they'll be able to change their partner to suit their idea of an ideal partner. As the saying goes, 'a leopard doesn't change its spots'. It is rare when a man decides to change his behaviour or attitude to suit his wife's ideals. In most cases, the man turns out to be set in his ways - often due to his ego or some other reason he deems to be genuine - and the lady ends up becoming miserable when she realises her hopes at finding someone she is compatible with have been shattered by her assumption that he would change.

There may have been a couple of cases where the man did change to become better, but those cases aren't the popular, oft-related stories. Since a lot of women are reactive in nature, she in turn may start to act badly in her bid to revenge the wrong, resulting in an impending disaster looming over their heads.

Accepting the proposal of someone who holds different values from you is like going into a transaction with exceedingly high hopes. You are more likely to end up disappointed and heartbroken. I know this because it's what happened to me.

It appeared that we weren't a good match, but I told myself, "He'll probably come to see things my way if he understands my reasons," amidst other excuses. The truth is, we didn't have the same level of exposure and understanding about life. My aspirations weren't in line with his; I wasn't ready to let go of my own ideals and he didn't understand why I seemed so determined to move my life forward, which is what I was trying to do.

Time seemed to be passing by, with me being in the same place, so I dared to change the status quo by actively working towards achieving my dreams and aspirations. In the end, I only had myself to blame as I was made to understand that I am a woman and women ought to make sacrifices for their marriages to work. That statement sounded ridiculous to me, as I didn't understand why it was okay for a man to be an achiever and a woman an onlooker. Aren't men also supposed to make sacrifices in marriage as well? For a marriage to work, it involves **both** parties to understand the importance of sacrifice, and requires **both** parties to actively work towards the success of the marriage.

Thus, the man you agree to settle with has to understand this concept of you both contributing and building the foundation of your marriage together, so you don't end up doing all the work and feeling burnt out, yet getting little or no appreciation for all your hard work.

From my knowledge of history, I remembered stories from the past where Muslim women were exceptionally amazing, so my dream had always been to join those women to leave my footsteps in the sands of time. Why, then, was I being made to accept that that dream of mine was only going to remain a dream - a figment of my imagination? It didn't make any sense to me, so I worked out ways to still go on and achieve, even when it meant going without for some time. In the end, it came down to choosing either your continuous success and growth, or risk having a broken home. *Allaahu musta'an.*

THE IMPORTANCE OF GOOD MANNERS IN A HUSBAND

So you've been searching for a long time and then you finally get to speak with this nice-looking brother who prays his salah, recites Qur'an with proper tajweed and has clean teeth, yet speaks to people disrespectfully, has no regards for other people's feelings, and actually sees no reason why a woman should voice her frustration even when she is hurting and looking to get married to him - my advice: RUN!

Do such people exist? Yes, they do!

Our Nabiy (sallAllaahu alayhi wasallam) said, "The only reason I have been sent is to perfect good manners."[10]

This hadith lays emphasis on the importance of good manners. Part of good manners is that we are mindful of how we treat others, take responsibility for our actions and own up to being wrong when we actually err. Treating one's spouse with respect and love makes the love that Allaah has placed in your hearts blossom.

Are you a sensitive person who pays attention to things around you and is self-conscious to the point that a misdirected outburst could ignite sparks of anger in you? Are you a shy person who easily gets embarrassed? Are you the very emotional type who finds it hard to stifle her anger when treated unjustly, irrespective of where you are? Then don't **ever** consider settling for the brother I painted in the above scenario, as such a union is headed for the bottom of the ocean even before it started.

In some cases, though, very poor manners are masked with the 'I am so quiet' or 'I can't even kill an ant' attitude. Trust me on this: he isn't going to be 'so quiet' when you both eventually marry, so, my dear, *wake up and smell the coffee*.

DON'T BE FOOLED BY OUTWARD PIETY

Do **not** be fooled by a 'holier-than-thou' attitude. Dig deep so you can uncover what is really in the parcel and not what the cover of the parcel tells you is in it. How many times have you bought a box of an item with the colour of the item in the box being different from the colour of the item displayed on the cover of the box? That has happened to me countless times. So pay attention to how he speaks to the doorman in the bank, the cleaner at the hospital or the person who mistakenly spilled mud-water on him whilst you were both waiting for a taxi.

How did he react with your nieces when they were screaming at the top of their voices whilst he was trying to have a civil conversation with someone on the phone?

10. Sahih al-Bukhari

How did he react to the bunch of teenagers who spoke rudely to him? All these things matter; our maturity or lack of it shines through when we are put on the spot in some of these cases I've mentioned.

My dear, do not turn a blind eye to any of these things as insignificant as they may seem, as these and many more incidents, will happen when you both eventually start living together; the way we treat people we feel are under us reveals our real personalities. If you want to know the true character of a person, study them when they have everything going well for them as well as when they have things going bad. A person's true character often shines through at these times. When you have everything, being arrogant comes easily to many except the one Allaah has saved from it.

It's important you know this as you will take up the role of both friend and critic if you both eventually go ahead and marry. In bad times, you'd know if he is the kind of person who gives up easily whilst ensuring everyone gets dragged along in his misery. This is significant because a little rough day at work has been known to lead to the end of some marriages. *Allaahu musta'an.*

Since the idea of courtship in Islam doesn't entail that you stay in close proximity for a long time, it then means you need to employ resources available to you - such as people around you who have had close dealings with him - to guide you on his true character.

In order to check if these people are being sincere, ask questions like, "If he was asking for the hand of your sister or daughter in marriage, would you give him?" Notice that most of the things I have mentioned here have to do with personality types; in other words, you both need to have complementary personalities. And even when there are slight differences, it is important the differences are not on fundamental issues that could make or mar the foundation of the marriage. When the foundation of a marriage is shaky, the likelihood of the marriage surviving the storm, rain, and blocks thrown at it are slim.

My du'a for you:
May Allaah (subhaanahu wa ta'ala) guide your steps as you make this important life decision. May He help you be firm upon goodness and guide you in making this choice that has a great influence over the rest of your life in this world and in the akhirah. May Allaah (subhaanahu wa ta'ala) guide your steps as you strive to ensure that this decision is made sincerely and totally for His sake. Aamiyn.

"If you had all relied on Allaah (subhaanahu wa ta'ala) as you should rely on Him, then He would have provided for you as He provides for the birds, who wake up hungry in the morning and return with full stomachs at dusk." [11]

POINTS TO PONDER:

Make a list of your character traits and ask people really close to you to make a list for you as well. Seeing what people think about you helps you know whether you understand your personality traits or not. It also helps you spot those things you are probably doing differently from your perception of yourself, and gives room for you to work on it.

Make a list of the character traits of your prospective spouse and cross-check it with yours to see if there are connecting points. If there are not, please bid him goodbye.

Try not to be overly emotional when you are in this decision-making stage; emotions can cloud your judgement and make you overlook character traits or red flags you normally would have noticed.

Ensure that through this whole process, you do not lower your standards or compromise your core values all in the name of being considerate. It's one thing to be considerate, it's another thing to settle.

More importantly, make lots of du'a and know that Allaah is the Hearer of all du'a.

11. Sunan at-Tirmidhi

SECTION 2:
AND THEY LIVED HAPPILY EVER AFTER

"When you marry a man (or woman), you marry the family as well, so be sure of where you rest your head for it contributes to how peaceful your 'sleep' will be."
- Aishah Adams

CHAPTER 1
THE HONEYMOON IS OVER AND REALITY SETS IN

'The honeymoon doesn't have to be over,' I thought to myself. 'Where did all the lovey-dovey feelings disappear to? What does the road ahead hold? Only Allaah knows. If we are this way barely a month into the marriage, what then will I see in future? I shudder to even think about it!'

For many, the honeymoon period is often the sweetest time in a marriage. The length of time varies from marriage to marriage; some have it for 1 year, some for 6 months, some for 1 month, and some for 1 hour! SubhanAllaah! Its variance is dependent on the personality of the couple coming together to live as one. Most times, we try to make good first impressions when we start spending time with people, hence the explanation for why everything seems to be rosy at the onset of a marriage. Being nasty isn't the first thing that crosses your mind, except in rare cases, for example if you were treated badly.

When you meet someone, being lovely and sweet is the natural way to behave, especially when the intention involves *nikah*. We all seem to be on our best behaviour at first; going to lengths to please - and this is good. After some time, reality sets in. The excitement that accompanies a new achievement or territory calms down and our natural self takes over. We are all imperfect beings and our imperfection starts to shine through. In our bid to bond with our 'better half', sometimes one's real self settles into a routine alien to the spouse, leading to the first point of discord. At this point there is no turning back - you either work on making it work or you let things get out of hand and you end up being miserable. Whatever you decide, know that you are responsible for how things move on from here. If you had skipped the steps before *nikah*, then you need a plan on how to work through these shockers or '*nikah* busters' as they appear.

My honeymoon barely lasted a month. I immediately knew I had made a mistake, accepting the proposal of one whose ideals and goals were far from mine shortly after we started living together. After being together for one month, I was sure I had made a mistake I couldn't retract - or so I thought at the time. Perhaps the reason why

I felt I had to live with this mistake was because I had lost something I considered really precious and I was never going to get it back; I felt I just had to deal. This made me become like an angry bird. I was trying to transfer the anger of making the wrong choice instead of trying to live with it and make the best of it. Perhaps the shattered dreams of the marriage that could have been left me broken-hearted.

Most of us women prepare for marriage having *The Little Mermaid* and *Prince Charming* idea of marriage. We read a lot of books, attend as many lectures as possible, and speak about marriage, yet when you get in to it, the reality pales in comparison to all you ever thought you'd meet. Sometimes a far cry, in fact!

MEN ARE SIMILAR

Having been at this stage at some point in my life and having tasted divorce, I have come to the conclusion that men have similar characteristics, they just differ in the degree. For example, all men have an ego; what makes one man better than the other is how he acknowledges this and acts on it. Some try to not strut about in arrogance all in the name of being created with an ego, others hide under it and commit all sorts of heinous crimes to justify their being macho. I guess it all depends on how you choose to relate with the most annoying traits you find in your spouse after marriage.

Reflecting back to the beginning of my marital journey, I realise I must have condemned the marriage for doom sooner than I should have. In my defence, however, our differences were too enormous and it broke my heart to accept the reality that our marriage was heading for the rocks. At first, I told myself I was probably being hasty and that this annoyance and anger I felt at giving myself to the most wrong person ever would go away and be replaced by the doting wifey love I had hoped would surge in my heart for my husband once I got to know him. It never really left me. In the end, I had to fight a constant battle within myself to accept the marriage and make the best of it.

Below are some key things you can work on as the reality of the marriage begins to dawn on you.

BE MINDFUL OF ALLAAH

Being mindful that Allaah will get you through both rough times and stormy tides that will rock your boat almost to a point of wrecking it. It is important that you make

the taqwa of Allaah the foundation of your home, as you will never go wrong when you do so. Such consciousness of Allaah will help you to forgive and let go when you feel *so* hurt that you can barely muster the strength to push on. It is that which will blow out the fires of revenge burning in your heart. The taqwa of Allaah can move mountains for you as Allaah (subhaanahu wa ta'ala) has said:
"... and whoever fears Allaah, He will make for him a way out." [12]

Marriage is a rose with thorns; its beauty does not deaden the sharpness of its thorns. Just like you would not throw away a rose because of its prickly thorns, do not rush to forfeit your marriage in the heat of the moment. With taqwa, you will be mindful of Allaah (subhaanahu wa ta'ala); and if you are mindful of Allaah in all endeavours in your marriage, you would have set a beautiful and strong foundation for the rest of your home to be built upon.

Consciousness of Allaah is what prevents you from setting traps for your spouse when you know they have stepped out of line and oppressed you. Being mindful of Allaah cannot be over emphasised as it is the bedrock of any successful venture - marriage, in this case.

My dear, put Allaah in charge of all your marital affairs and you will find peace and tranquillity in your relationship with your spouse. Do not let the constant arguments with your spouse or squabbles with in-laws stop you from relating with them with taqwa of Allaah (azza wa jaal).

There are going to come times when it will feel like you made the worst mistake ever by agreeing to marry this man you call 'husband'. At those times, remind yourself of Allaah's promises for the patient, then strive not to go overboard in your anger and despair. Our Lord never sleeps and He is in control of all affairs.

COMMUNICATION
The beginning and end of any marriage is held by the presence or absence of effective communication between the couple. How many times have issues been swept under the rug in a bid to avoid a fight?

Please do not let the fear of disagreement between you and your spouse come in the way of you communicating your grievances and heartache to him. Strive to present your pain about his actions or inactions in the best of manners. Be open and fully

---

12. Surah at-Talaq: 2

present when communicating any pain you're feeling, but don't feel downtrodden if this openness isn't reciprocated.

SEX

This is very important for the success and growth of any marriage; unfortunately, many of us have great challenges in this area and don't communicate our frustrations to the one person who must know them: our spouse!

How many marriages have collapsed because their sex life was a pitiful sight? It becomes even more frustrating if, like me, you keep yourself for 'the one' and then realise your dreams about having a beautiful sex life with your 'beloved' has stayed a fantasy.

No matter the challenges you encounter in this important aspect of your marriage, strive hard to improve it. Read as many books as possible, consult a therapist or marriage coach, speak to your husband, and by all means, work on it! Do not ever underestimate the importance of sex in the overall success of your marriage. Find ways to spice up this aspect of your marriage even when it feels like that is the only bit of your marriage that is working.

Sometimes we do not realise that an over-hyped fight is due to a result of poor marital relations between a couple. How many times have you seen a rather flimsy issue cause a huge battle? It is often an aftermath of a bigger problem: intimacy challenges.

Try to find out ways to bring back love and life into your intimacy with your spouse. Work hard at not letting barriers be built as it's usually harder to pull them down once they've been erected. I'm still working hard to bring down the walls I put up during the tumultuous period following my honeymoon phase, but it's my aim to obliterate them all.

TEETHING PERIOD OF MARRIAGE

My dear sister, understand that every marriage has its teething period. This is usually a period of severe turmoil; a phase where you would ask yourself several times, "How did I get myself into this mess?" "How did I not notice he was like this or like that?" A lot of self-criticism will arise, but remember that sometimes even after we have done all the research needed, the ability to make the right decision is in the hands of Allaah, for He alone is the Best of those who guide.

This teething period varies in length from one marriage to the other. Some experience it for 7 years, others for 10 years; some have it for 3 years. For most, though, the first 5-7 years are often very tough. Constant fights and squabbles is the order of the day; if these fights are not well-managed, it could lead to divorce, and in the not-so-fatal cases, complete breakdown in communication between the couple. Even the best of couples may feel they made a wrong choice of partner during this phase, so what about the mismatched couples? They feel even worse! This is a very sensitive period of the marriage and you can get through this phase with patience and applying reason in all you do.

It is vital that you remain steadfast and do not despair of the mercy of Allaah at this point. Many have lost their deen or their strong stance on the deen as a result of marital issues they faced during the teething phase. Please don't be one of them. It is exceptionally easy to fall into despair at this point as the sharp contrast between the honeymoon period and the teething phase is often too much for the one who has to go through it.

I found it hard to deal with this sharp contrast as well. At first it felt like movie magic, like I was only imagining the honeymoon phase of our marriage. I used to think to myself, "How did the supposedly loving spouse become this mean and oppressive?" "Where did the antagonism come from?" These are just a couple of the many more questions I thought about a lot of the time. In the end, I decided to take it a day at a time, make the best of each day, and let the day's troubles set with the sun. This restored sanity back into my life and marriage and helped me feel more confident in my worship of Him.

Through it all I used to remind myself of the love of Allaah and His promise for those who are patient. I also used to carry my heart burdens to Allaah, knowing He alone was the Comforter and He alone was the One that would bring me out from what seemed like a dark tunnel. Though things have quietened down in my current marriage, I have stuck to this practice so I don't become lax and get any more surprises as I'm not sure I have the strength for any more relationship drama.

The transition from being single to the complexities of being married can be really tough, especially when as a woman. Intending to make the best out of whatever situation you are presented with in the marriage is what differentiates one marriage from another. Hold on firmly to Al-Waduud, be prepared to work hard at making the marriage work, and have *yaqeen* - full, unshakeable certainty -that He will bless your home with goodness.

POINTS TO PONDER:

Be prepared to see a flip in the coin upon marriage. If you do, take comfort in knowing that every marriage has its own challenges.

If you experience a flip of your marriage coin, hold on firmly to the rope of Allaah - He is the only One who can see you through the rough patches.

Be mindful of Allaah in your relationship with your spouse and have full certainty that He will see you through thick and thin.

Open the lines of communication in all spheres of your life with your spouse; a breakdown in communication has been known to cause rifts in many marriages.

Sex - the rarely spoken about topic - is a must-have in marriage and is the most important area. Getting it wrong in this department could make or mar your marital life, thus I encourage you to work hard to ensure it's interesting and fun.

CHAPTER 2
MANAGING EXPECTATIONS IN MARRIAGE

So you've been married for a period of time, and at this point, reality has set in and you now know the truth about your chosen spouse. What do you do with the cards displayed right in front of you? You work on making the best of your cards to attain the success you want. Life is not a bed of roses without thorns; as beautiful as it can be, there are thorns. What you need to ask yourself is whether you are going to throw away the roses because of the thorns or whether you are going to enjoy the beauty of the roses and endure the jabs of the thorns when they eventually prick you. This is what managing your expectations is all about.

After a short while of being married, I realised I didn't have a choice but to accept the choice of partner I had made no matter how much it broke my heart. It constantly felt like I had jeopardised my future due to haste, and I didn't want to believe he wouldn't change, but the reality was that things seemed to be getting worse. The miscarriages I was suffering didn't make things any easier. There were days I'd sit and think that perhaps the fights were partly the reason for Allaah not blessing me with a child yet - I either fix the mess I was in or risk being childless, as good is from Allaah and evil is from that which our hands have sent forth.

Knowing what I know now, below are some of the things I came to later understand I could have done to ease and aid my circumstances.

BEFORE YOU ACT: WHAT DOES ALLAAH EXPECT OF ME?

It is important that we realise we are ambassadors of Islam and how we act affects the general view non-Muslims, as well as nominal Muslims, have of us.

There was once a couple who were having a heated argument at home. Coincidentally, the mother of the groom was staying over, so she intervened and the disagreement was resolved. At some point, she was reported to have said, "I can't believe you and my son, who appear to have a better understanding of Islam, are behaving this way."

This struck a chord as it made the couple realise the enormity of their actions.

We have to constantly ask ourselves what Islam expects of us. We are not infallible, so it is inevitable that we will make mistakes now and then. The realisation of the high status we hold in our communities should aid us to constantly improve ourselves and in turn, improve our relationship with our spouse.

The home is the bedrock of all societies, and as such, we need to work on having well-formed and thriving families so that we can build strong and peaceful communities. It's for this reason that we always need to call ourselves to account with the question, *What does Allaah expect of me?*

Each time you get annoyed by something your spouse does, ask yourself, *What is expected of me?* When you are being unjustly treated by your in-laws, your response to such actions should be based on your answer to this important question as well. When your husband favours your co-wife over you in a polygynous marriage, your actions should be based on your answer to, *What is expected of me?* When your step-children act in an unruly manner due to the influence of their mum, your response to their actions should be based on this question as well.

What is expected of me? Am I being a good ambassador of Islam? Am I acting on the knowledge Allaah has blessed me with, or am I acting contrary to that knowledge? Though it is impossible to maintain a high standard of good character at all times, being mindful of your role in the community helps to mould your character, and more importantly, your character with your spouse.

Once I had to address a young couple intending on marriage and I reminded them that Allaah says about the couple in the Qur'an: "They are a clothing for you and you are clothing for them."[13]

Clothes do not only cover up your beauty, they also cover up your defects. So the one who is most likely to see you in all your glory - both strengths and flaws - is your spouse. The onus thus lies on you both to strive to screen each other's faults and strive to manage as much as you can within the limits of Islam.

When an item of clothing does not cover us properly, it becomes imperative that we either try to 'mend' it so it fulfils its role, or we dispose of it when it shows clear signs of doing other than what it is meant to do. Being an 'ill fit' is often one of the main causes

---

13. Surah al-Baqarah: 187

of divorce, thus it is important that you strive to be a good cover for your spouse.

STOP USING VERSES OF THE QUR'AN TO JUSTIFY FOOLISH ACTIONS

When you err or make terrible mistakes, please do not justify your mistakes with the Qur'an and ahadith. For instance, it's common to find a man oppressing his wife or beating her to a pulp, quickly hide behind Qur'anic traditions, despite being ignorant of their *tafsir*!

I am yet to come across any hadith narrating to us an incident in which the Nabiy (sallAllaahu alayhi wasallam) beat any of his wives. In fact, we have narrations in which he condemned beating a wife in the day and intending to sleep with her at night, so why then do we allow ourselves to be brainwashed with these justifications? Perhaps it is due to our limited knowledge of the deen that has led us to believe anything shoved at us in the name of religion. A solution to this is clear: Invest your time seeking knowledge of the deen, strive to have up-to-date information about rulings on different topics as they affect day-to-day life with your spouse. This way, you know what is what and no one can concoct any cock-and-bull story when they want to treat you unjustly.

Another oft-quoted verse used to justify oppressive behaviour by men is: 'Arrijalun qawaamuna 'alaa nisaa',[14] which means: 'Men are the protectors (and maintainers) of women'. If you are asked to protect something, are you supposed to be the one harming that thing? Sadly, this is often the case, whether intentionally or otherwise; leading to the collapse of the one whom they were supposed to protect and love. May Allaah save you from such fate.

In the event that this is the current situation in your home at the moment, please do not despair. **Understand that Allaah is not unaware of your efforts and it is He who will turn around your challenges and bring out much good from them.**

My dear, it is important you seek knowledge, as it empowers and lights your path. Seek knowledge of the deen, make research about any questionable sounding quotation presented to you, and please do not justify your flaws with Qur'anic traditions. Just as you're working on yourself, do not give room for anyone to oppress you in the name of Islam.

---

11. Surah an-Nisa: 34

BE SMART

Have you ever had to live with someone whose annoying character turns your stomach, yet you have to relate with the person as they are supposedly your 'better half'? Well I had to! I think back to that time and I don't understand how I stuck it out in that marriage for so long. The marriage lasted for almost three years, and when it eventually ended, it was almost like I had been let loose from a cage! *SubhanAllaah*.

If you find yourself in a similar situation, do not allow yourself to become depressed as a result of all the issues arising - take a step back, stop and breathe. Then look at the situation you are in critically and think about it rationally. How can you make the best of what you have? How can you work with what you have to achieve what you want? How can you dampen this feeling of defeat engulfing your heart?

Perhaps you need to reset your expectations and dwell in the present rather than what could have been. Do not focus on other people's relationships as it could cause you a lot of heartache and longing to change the status quo. Remember that the grass always looks greener on the other side until you draw close and realise that what appeared to be grass is a mere mirage.

Focus on making the best of what you have - invest your time in making du'a to Allaah and researching ways to make your personality type co-exist with your spouse's personality type in harmony. Read books on marital harmony written by both Muslims and non-Muslims alike.
Some books that come readily to mind that I gained benefit from are:
• *The Surrendered Wife* by Laura Doyle
• *The 5 Love Languages* by Gary Chapman
• *The Marriage of Your Dreams* by Rick Johnson
• *Men are like Waffles, Women are like Spaghetti* by Bill Farrel and Pam Farrel
• *Is that all He Thinks About?* by Marla Taviano
• *When a Woman Inspires Her Husband* by McMenamin Cindi

Work on your emotional intelligence and work on keeping your tongue tied when you are upset, as this is a department a lot of us women lack control in. Being angry is human, being able to keep one's tongue in check distinguishes a consciously-aware Muslim from the pack. May Allaah grant us success. Aamiyn.

Instead of exploding in anger in your husband's face, how about going into an empty room and speaking to yourself loud enough for you to hear, but low enough to not be overheard? The room used for such purpose is often referred to as a 'war room'.

Likewise, you could find an activity that helps you let off steam and engage in it. A friend of mine once told me that working out helped her let off steam and focus her energy on the obstacle ahead. Some even take to writing or journaling - I fall in this category - as writing can be extremely therapeutic. It is a great tool for self-healing and reflection. Sometimes, writing letters to people who hurt us can be helpful, even if you don't end up sending the letters. It helps you get all of your emotions out on paper and relieves stress and anxiety.

Another aspect of being smart is to avoid displaying your dirty linen in public. No matter what happens between you and your spouse, strive hard not to sing your husband's flaws to all and sundry. After you forget the episode, others probably will *not* forget; thus you would have created a bad impression of him in places you probably wouldn't want him to be disrespected. When you feel choked up and you need to let off steam, walk or write it off.

In your moments of reflection, consider ways you can help him learn how to treat you by being the example you would like him to be. This is easier said than done, BUT… if you are able to apply yourself to tasks in this way, it will aid you in putting down a good foundation for your marriage. Be selfless for the sake of Allaah, but do not expect too much from your spouse, so that you don't set yourself up for dissappointment. Allaah says:
"And the servants of the Most Merciful are those who walk upon the earth easily, and when the ignorant address them [harshly], they say [words of] peace." [15]

This is not to say your spouse is foolish, it just means they are acting poorly and when they do, you do not respond by acting like them. Instead, strive to be the bigger person and teach them the right thing to do through your character. Actions are usually more powerful than empty words.

POINTS TO PONDER:
Focus on trying to improve yourself and not your spouse; change towards success starts from you.

Repel evil with good; being treated badly is not an excuse to act poorly as well.

Focus on your relationship and not on the relationship of others, as all that glitters is not gold.

---

15. Surah al-Furqan: 63

Stop focusing on what could have been; instead try to make the best of what is…

Trust in Allaah and refer all matters to Him; indeed, He is able to do all things.

CHAPTER 3
FLIGHT OR SABR - WHICH WAY TO GO?

So you've been working hard at managing your expectations; better still you've used every tip in the book to make it work, yet things seem rather gloomy with no sign of a silver lining. How does one proceed? Are you going to manage his faults or are you going to work yourself out of the marriage?

It's a fact of life that there comes a period in marriages when you have to sit down and decide your line of action, after all is said and done. Be sure not to make this decision when you are in an emotional state, as you are more likely to make the wrong decision. The emotion, be it anger, disappointment, or grief will eventually pass, but the effects of your decision will stay with you - forever. Remember this. Think carefully about how you choose to continue so you don't look back and lament on what could have been. I have seen far too many older women feel this way about their marriage. Their defence for the better part is usually, "I made the sacrifices for my children." It's beautiful to be selfless, but not when it becomes injurious to you and all that you believe in and stand for. You can't give love that you don't have.

The problem with being vulnerable sometimes is that when you have invested emotions in the institution and nothing seems to be forthcoming, your emotions might come crashing down in such a way that you might never be able to completely fit the pieces together. Sometimes, though, you need to understand that being vulnerable in a marriage is not necessarily for your partner; it's more for you. Invest yourself, live life, and don't just exist. Hurt and heal. More importantly, show up every time, irrespective of what is thrown at you.

It's about how you show up in the marriage and fulfil your share of the bargain. You can be vulnerable and yet have little or no expectations of your husband. **Being vulnerable and having high expectations don't necessarily need to be closed sets.** It doesn't mean that the moment you do not show up like you are expected to, all your efforts are futile. No. Just show up and strive to hold up your end of the bargain and work on not focusing on whether he does or does not.

Irrespective of his actions, strive to bring forth your best traits when you are with him. Allaah will not question you about what he did or did not do, instead He (subhaanahu wa ta'ala) will question you about that which your own hands send forth. Do not beat yourself up if the high standards you have set for yourself and spouse are not fulfilled. This shouldn't be the basis for taking flight in the event you are getting too choked and frustrated, as I was at one point in my marriage.

Work on communicating things to him as you see them, as it's common to discover your spouse did not realise the enormity of his actions. Perhaps he is looking at things as 'no big deal' and you are almost turning blue-black from anger at his lack of care and concern for things that are going on between you both, and for your home.

Accompany patience with lots of excuses for your spouse. There are a number of times I have harboured a grudge against my husband, only to find out he didn't intend things the way I was thinking, or perhaps he didn't see it through the lens I saw it through. Again, invest your time in learning daily. You'll be amazed at how many resources are out there in the form of books, lectures, videos and podcasts to assist the one truly seeking.

In the event you decide to take flight, then know that we have very judgemental people in our society and their judgement towards the plight of divorcees is really pathetic; you might need to waddle through the water with little or no support. Sometimes though, the intensity of the problems could be due to a lack of understanding of your spouse - with a little patience here and a little patience there, things could eventually turn around for the best.

Should you eventually decide to go the flight route, make loads of du'a and have full certainty in the acceptance of your du'a. If your reason for deciding to opt out is genuine and sincere, you would find help in re-settling down from places you never imagined for indeed Allaah is the Controller of the hearts of mankind and He (azza wa jaal) can turn them in whichever direction He pleases.

LEAVING AN ABUSIVE MARRIAGE

There are many women in abusive marriages who are holding on due to the inability to face the enormity of the consequences of leaving. Please don't be one of those. **When you stay on in an abusive relationship - whether verbally, emotionally, or physically abusive - it's almost as though you are teaching those around you to embrace the oppression,** especially when there are children present. It's almost as if you are saying, 'It's not a problem to allow my spouse to abuse me'. This is not okay.

It's about you examining yourself and saying, "Am I going to stay and NOT complain or am I just going to pack up and leave as this doesn't seem to be working?" Complaining doesn't serve your situation is a positive way; you have the opportunity and the full right to do something about the status quo. Sadly, not all women can just walk away for many practical reasons. In such cases, it's vital they ask themselves, *How does a woman who values herself act?* Step back, breathe, and decide what you **really** want.

You have to decide what you are going to turn a blind eye to and re-evaluate your values to see if you are upholding them. What can you bear? What can you handle? Be true to yourself. **Do not make the decision based on what your parents would say, or what your friends would say, or what society would say. Remember: this is your life and how you run it is consequential to YOU.** At the end of the day you're the one living in the marriage every single day; either earning Allaah's pleasure or earning His wrath, and we seek refuge in Allaah that the latter is the case in your marriage.

I think coming to terms with the fact that it was my life, and that my choices were mostly going to affect me, informed my insistence to call it quits with my ex when he raised his hands to me. At first, the pool of sentiments swam before my eyes and I was hesitant; but when I flashed back to all that had happened before the last fight and what I had had to endure over the years all in the name of 'sucking it in', I had to be true to myself. I had made a huge mistake.

I had to say to myself, "Yes, you made a big mistake marrying this guy, and yes, you have made many other mistakes; but you have been trying to fill a *basket* with water! It's not going to get filled, hence you are going to remain miserable. The rest of your life is a long time, so why jeopardise that in the name of 'what people will say'?"

After having this hard talk with myself, I made up my mind, took my stance and stuck with it. Alhamdulillah. That was the right thing I did back then. Perhaps I should have 'womaned up' sooner; whatever the case may have been then, it's different now. The die had been cast and life must go on.

If you choose to stay and bear your circumstances, aim to avoid complaining about the decision you have made. If you find that you truly can't bear it without complaints, it means you can't bear it at all, so be brave and take the high road so you can move on.

Be clear and real with yourself. Perhaps you need to ask yourself, 'Can I do this for the next 2 years? Can I do this for another 5 years? Do I see myself enduring this for the rest of my life? Is this going to kill me if I stay for another year? Can I even stick it out for another week?' Silence or a decision to stay is a decision in and of itself, so if you are not trying to change anything about your current situation, then it means you are okay with how things are.

Whatever you decide to do in the end, examine yourself and be sure of how you want to proceed. This is basically for you to take charge of your life and move it in the direction you are sure you want it to go, and of course make du'a once you have made up your mind and trust that He will help you through it all.

May Allaah grant you wisdom to make the right decision and ease in accepting His decree whether in things we like or in things we detest, as Allaah says:
"But perhaps you hate a thing and it is good for you; and perhaps your love a thing and it is bad for you. And Allaah knows, while you know not." [16]

Therefore, tie your camel, then put your trust in Allaah.

POINTS TO PONDER:

The decision to leave or stay is in your hands; do not let your worry over others' criticism stop you from what you believe to be the best for you.

Irrespective of what people say; purify your intentions and take action.

Do not stay on in an abusive relationship - doing so would only send the wrong waves to people around.

16. Surah al-Baqarah: 216

SECTION 3:
WHEN THE CHIPS ARE DOWN

"I told you I'd move on. I told you I'd let you go someday. Honestly, it was the hardest thing I've ever done but it was worth it. For me, for my heart. You hurt me so bad. You killed my trust, you changed me. I knew I could be strong enough to let you go. I knew it and I did it. I can't explain how proud I am. Because I'm the only one who knows how much you hurt me. But here I am now, healing. We may love the wrong person, cry for the wrong person, but one thing is sure, mistakes will help us find the right person someday." - *Unknown*

"Sometimes people with the worst past create the best future."
- *Umar ibn Al-Khattab (radiyAllaahu anhu)*

CHAPTER 1
EMOTIONAL ISSUES
SURROUNDING DIVORCE

"I divorce you," he said to me over the phone and I thought, 'SubhanAllaah! Not again!' I immediately burst into tears and begged him and reminded him of the sacrifices I had made with the hope that it would soften his heart and make him rescind on his stance to end the marriage. Here I was miles away from home, trying hard to focus on my purpose for being away from my beloved family only to have this thrown at me. For me it was a case of, 'After all I had done to make this marriage work, it still comes to this? Why then did I make all the sacrifices I'd made in the past?'

I asked him, "What is the basis of this pronouncement?"
"You are a bad mother!"

My jaw dropped.
"How so?" I asked, close to tears.
"How could you leave her with me and go away?"

I remember running downstairs with tears streaming down my eyes as I tried to get my sisters to say something to me that would calm me down as the shock of the pronouncement was too much for me.

On hearing the excuse he gave for the pronouncement, I thought to myself, 'Wasn't it you who coerced me and encouraged me to go, promising to bring our child to join me, and making me feel that I was actually making a worthy sacrifice for my family? How did the story suddenly change?' After all, he had our child - *his* child - with him and it appeared like I wasn't going to have access to her. Allaah (subhaanahu wa ta'ala) is the Hearer of du'a and it was He who restored my child back to me and finally helped me get through the darkest tunnel of my life following the oppressive divorce I suffered at the hands of one who I foolishly entrusted with my life and the life of my child.

It's been a couple of years since the incident, but the enormity of the betrayal stills rings a bell in my head any time I remember it. Sometimes I think, *how could I have made a wrong choice of spouse to make myself and my family have to suffer so much?* but then I immediately remind myself that one mistake doesn't deface a person's life if they do not let it. Besides, there's an adage in my native language that says *'ninu ikoko dudu nii ekoo funfun tin jade'* which translates to 'the creamy oats come out from a black pot'. This means the fact that a person has bad roots doesn't necessarily mean they will turn out bad. In Shaa Allaah, this would not mar my life or that of my beloved family.

DIVORCE IS A WEIGHTY THING

Divorce is accompanied by a myriad of emotions. Sometimes the emotions are so strong that one can almost choke from the intensity of it, especially when you know you invested so much in the marriage and it still ended. People do not plan to become divorced when they marry; for a lot of women, they go into it thinking they'd be with their partner for the rest of their life, taking care of him and having a beautiful family. You know that 'and they lived happily ever after' fairy tale is what many hope for before venturing into the 'land of the unknown' - at least that was what I hoped for when I was going to embark on the journey of marriage.

In the event of a break up, women tend to suffer the most, especially because of their attachment to the family and nurturing a conducive environment for the growth of their children.

The deep emotional pain that accompanies this sad incident is often too much to handle. Some don't ever recover from it. One's self esteem is often badly affected, particularly in many of our patriarchal communities where women are almost often treated like doormats.

What amazes me though, is the attitude of the womenfolk to their fellow women going through the pain of divorce.

SubhanAllaah! They tend to be so judgemental, looking down their high horses at the ones going through the trial, which further heightens the sinking feeling for the one already struggling through the ocean of pain. *Allaahu musta'an.*

It takes great strength for one to be able to pull themselves from the abyss, and the struggle to achieve balance in one's life again is real. This balance is even harder to achieve for those who have had children, particularly when the children are still quite young, or in cases where one or more of the children have certain special health conditions. The help of Allaah is sought from falling into this sort of trial.

When one is in this place of pain, all sorts of thoughts comes to mind as Shaytan is happy to befriend you at times like this. Allaah forbid, you act on any of those errant thoughts that plague you at this time. These horrible thoughts range from wishing bad things (even death) to happen to the ex, or wishing to commit suicide or harm oneself in bid to get the attention of people or of one's ex. Emotions can be overwhelmingly powerful, that is why it is important to turn to Allaah (subhaanahu wa ta'ala) at times of heightened emotions like this.

Allaah (subhaanahu wa ta'ala) says:
"And whoever fears Allaah, He will make for him a way out." [17]

Notice that this verse was revealed in Surah at-Talaq! Is not Allaah indeed The Wise? Having taqwa of Allaah is one of the things to firmly hold onto so one does not fall deeper into the abyss of despair. Acting on any of the many errant thoughts that crosses one's mind when in this state of pain is tantamount to pushing one's self deeper into the chasm of agony and despair, as sin does not beget anything other than regret and despair.

It is important to state at this point that whilst it is better for each couple to work to heal a marriage that is hurting them and their loved ones, it's also of great importance that we know that sometimes some marriages cannot be healed even when abuse is not involved. Some people are determined not to settle for anything less than the standards they have set for their life and it's wrong to judge them if you decide to stay put doing something or being with someone that is helping you constantly earn Allaah's displeasure. We have to be kind to ourselves and acknowledge the fact that we haven't been created by Allaah to live unhappily.

This brings to mind the hadith of Ibn Abbas (radiyAllaahu anhu):
The wife of Thabit bin Qais came to the Prophet (sallAllaahu alayhi wasallam) and said, "O, Allaah's Messenger (sallAllaahu alayhi wasallam)! I do not blame Thabit for defects in his character or his religion, but I, being a Muslim, dislike to behave in un-Islamic manner (if I remain with him)." On that Allaah's Messenger (sallAllaahu alayhi wasallam) said (to her), "Will you give back the garden which your husband has given you (as mahr)?" She said, "Yes." Then the Prophet (sallAllaahu alayhi wasallam) said to Thabit, "O, Thabit! Accept your garden, and divorce her once."

---

17. Surah at-Talaq: 2

DIVORCE HAS ITS STAGES

I once read an article written by a sister who had just suffered a loss and I remember her writing that psychologists say there is a cycle one goes through when one suffers a loss. Note that this 'cycle' isn't one of those cycles we study in biology about photosynthesis or digestion et al; it is an emotional cycle connected to loss.

At first, you tell yourself it didn't happen - you'll wake up and think it was all a dream. In the event you were pushing for the divorce due to all you suffered in the marriage, you still don't get to skip this step. In fact, you start by wishing you'd wake up and realise you didn't make the mistake of marrying someone you had no similarities with. The more celibate you were before marriage, the more painful this cycle gets.

"I divorce you." Those were the words that woke me up from the deep slumber I had been in since the recent events that culminated in the pronouncement. Before then, I was just sitting down by my phone, hoping and praying Allaah would touch his heart and make him stand by his word - a promise he made to me before I packed my bags to go on my trip.

Little did I know that the journey I was about to go on would be a long journey, one in which I would never have the opportunity to go back to the starting point. *QadarAllaahu wa maa shaa af'ala.* We plan and Allaah plans, and He (subhaanahu wa ta'ala) is the Best of Planners.

Allaah (subhaanahu wa ta'ala) says:
"And if Allaah should touch you with adversity, there is no remover of it except Him. And if He touched you with good, then He is over all things competent; and He is the subjugator over His servants. And He is Wise, the Acquainted [with all]." [18]

Also, in a hadith narrated by Abu al-'Abbas 'Abdullah bin 'Abbas (radiyAllaahu anhu), the Nabiy (sallAllaahu alayhi wasallam) was reported to have said:
"Young man, I will teach you some words. Be mindful of God, and He will take care of you. Be mindful of Him, and you shall find Him at your side. If you ask, ask of God. If you need help, seek it from God. **Know that if the whole world were to gather together in order to help you, they would not be able to help you except if God had written so.** And if the whole world were to gather together in order to harm you, they would not harm you except if God had written so. The pens have been lifted, and the pages are dry." [19]

18. Surah al Anfam: 17-18
19. Sunan at-Tirmidhi

With the realisation of this important concept came acceptance of the trial that had struck and at some point patience followed it. **Being accepting of the decree of Allaah (subhaanahu wa ta'ala) is the way to go for anyone going through divorce or any other trial.** The hadith above was one I constantly reminded myself of whenever any errant thought came to my mind. I used to say to myself, 'Allaah is not unaware of my travails'.

I came to learn that the 'cycle' my friend had told me about was indeed the 5 stages of loss and grief: denial and isolation, anger, bargaining, depression, and finally, acceptance. Be grateful if you have the blessing of getting to the last stage, for many are not afforded this opportunity.

DENIAL AND ISOLATION

In this phase, you find yourself still using the word 'husband' to refer to your ex as it's new territory for you and the enormity of what has happened hasn't truly sunk in. Many women who have had divorce sprung on them will tell themselves that they'll wake up from this dream and realise it was just a small fight and that things will go back to how they were before the pronouncement. If you are fortunate to be around him, then perhaps there's the opportunity to still see him and work on patching things up as is the wisdom behind the 'iddah - waiting period - for the divorced woman.

The waiting period is supposed to be a time when you can both reconsider what you are about to do as well as be sure you really want to go ahead. For those like me, who were far away at the time of pronouncement, being allowed to do the 'iddah as prescribed by our deen becomes even harder. This inability to patch things up as a result of observing the 'iddah outside the house of the husband further heightens the pain.

Through it all, holding on to Allaah is what gets you through the severest of pain. Allaah is indeed Merciful and Compassionate to those who rely upon Him.

ANGER

At this point, you are still struggling with understanding why the divorce had to go through and why he didn't have more patience with you. This anger phase lingers for a while depending on the resources available to one in terms of support and counselling. It's a scary phase as well because at this point, a number of murderous thoughts crosses the mind and only a reminder of what acting on those thoughts could bring on stalls the action.

It is important to surround oneself with people upon the truth, friends and people of knowledge who are able to remind one to fear Allaah and not act irresponsibly due to a pain that would only be temporary.

BARGAINING

This phase sometimes comes before suffering a loss. In fact, in the event that this occurs after the loss, it is an attempt to negotiate the pain away. It's almost similar to the denial phase except that you are closer to accepting the truth of what has happened to you.

When I had to go through my divorce experience, I didn't really dwell in this phase. I was in denial for a really long time, by the time I got to this phase, I moved on quickly, but I didn't get to move on until I had tried filling the vacuum of hurt with remembrance of Allaah, acts of service to Allaah, and learning about the stories of the prophets and how they coped with their own trials.

DEPRESSION

Depression is a major mental disorder that is quite common, yet serious, as it leads to mood changes. It affects how you think, feel, and handle your daily activities which include, but are not limited to eating, sleeping, or working. According to the National Institute of Mental Health (NIMH) booklet, for one to be diagnosed with depression, the symptoms must be present persistently for at least two weeks and must have caused clinically significant distress and impairment.

When the reality of one's situation begins to dawn, you find yourself settling into this deep place of depression, except for the one to whom Allaah grants ease in conquering the pain. This depression can linger for a long time, and a number of people find it hard getting back to being themselves after this episode of immense agony and betrayal. Take note of changes you notice in your behavioural pattern, especially if someone else points them out to you. And do not delay in seeking help to get you through.

ACCEPTANCE

Rejoice if you are able to get to this phase at all. It takes a lot for a good number of women to reach this phase, and is achieved by the few fortunate ones. Some just settle into depression and fluctuate between a deep level of it and an attempt to push themselves towards accepting the reality of the trial that has stuck.

With the acknowledgement that Allaah is not unaware of your trials, comes patience and acceptance of His Decree. Allaah chose to try you with divorce, *Alhamdulilaah 'alaa kulli haal*. Indeed, He is worthy of praise in all circumstances.

It could have been worse. You could have remained married and lost your sight or embraced disbelief towards the end of your life. You could have died in one of the fights you had with your spouse or mistakenly hit him in a place that could have rendered him brain-dead. You could have engaged in a fight and whilst unknown to you both some electrical appliances could have set the home on fire until it was too late. Anything could have happened that could have been worse than this divorce, so strive to be thankful to Allaah, as much as you can as you accept that worse trials could have befallen you.

You should then follow up this thankfulness with loads and loads of istighfaar - seeking of forgiveness - for Allaah says:
"Ask forgiveness of your Lord. Indeed, He is ever a Perpetual Forgiver; He will send [rain from] the sky upon you in [continuing] showers; And give you increase in wealth and children and provide for you gardens and provide for you rivers." [20]

With His forgiveness comes blessings in abundance, as indicated by this verse. These blessings come in all forms - wealth, good health, success in all aspects of your life. Would you not then hurry to bow before the Most High who created us from nothing and to whom is our final return? Would you not lean on the One whose support suffices?

Following thankfulness and istighfaar is *sabr* - patience. When we make du'a we often present our heartaches before Al-Mujeeb, trusting and hoping He attends to our plea; now He will answer our cry as He (azza wa jaal) has said:
"And when My servants ask you [O, Muhammad], concerning Me - indeed I am near. I respond to the invocation of the supplicant when he calls upon Me. So let them respond to Me [by obedience] and believe in Me that they may be [rightly] guided." [21]

20. Surah Nuh: 10-12
21. Surah al Baqarah: 186

Believe in His abilities to respond to your supplication and strive to be patient even when it feels like you are choking on the intensity of the pain. No matter how stormy the clouds become, trust in Allaah and know that He is the Lord of the worlds. Sometimes you'd pray so hard for something, yet it doesn't seem like it's going to happen; have sabr. Allaah's delays are not denials. Sometimes the delay is actually to test our faith. As Allaah says:

"[He] who created death and life to test you [as to] which of you is best in deeds - and He is the Exalted in Might, the Forgiving." [22]

Trials and tribulations are synonymous to our existence. Divorce, like any other trial we face in life, tests our patience and faith greatly. The delayed response to our supplication further heightens the pain of the trial as we are often helpless at times like this. Take your strength from patience and total reliance on Allaah (subhaanahu wa ta'ala) and know that indeed, He is the Disposer of Affairs for those who believe and persevere.

Verily, Allaah is with you and He is the Guardian of those who believe and put their trust in Him, and He reminds us, *"So be patient with gracious patience."* [23]

POINTS TO PONDER:

Divorce, though painful could be a means of goodness for the one going through it if they approach the trial with the right attitude.

There are 5 stages of grief; do not beat yourself up when going through these phases.

Turn to Allaah in repentance and have certainty that He will grant you ease.

Ask for forgiveness and show a lot of gratitude to Allaah for verily it could have been worse.

22. Surah al-Mulk, 2
23. Surah al-Ma'arij, 5

CHAPTER 2
CULTURAL ISSUES ARISE AS WELL

"Why did you ask for a divorce? You should have been patient", "Don't you know the society will start to count the number of spouses you've had?", "Don't you know no one would be willing to marry someone who has already given birth?" The list of jabs from people is endless.

The effect of cultural ideologies on those dealing with the aftermath of a broken marriage is phenomenal. Our cultural beliefs have made it increasingly difficult to be empathetic towards other people's travails, which worsens the emotional state of the one already struggling to keep afloat due to the enormous weight of emotions they are dealing with.

There are a lot of cultural issues associated with divorce; sometimes the enormity of these cultural matters is what prevents many from being able to overcome the trauma of divorce or abusive marriages. These issues also push some divorcees to rush into a second mistake that could have been avoided in the absence of cultural pressures. Likewise, several women have stayed in abusive marriages because they fear a cultural repercussion. They are led to feel that being at the mercy of their husband is far better than coping with the judgemental jabs from all and sundry when they eventually summon up the courage to step out.

I experienced most of the cultural discrimination hinted above and much more. My divorce opened the door to disrespect and humiliation from people, causing some of my supposed close friends at the time to join the bandwagon of those dishing out insults. I can recall when the mother of one whom I believed to be close to me sent me a message that was so horrible, I couldn't help but burst into tears. In her text message she implied that she didn't want me at her daughter's house, especially as her daughter's husband was in no need of a second wife. The weight of the past weeks of *'iddah* suddenly felt too heavy for my shoulders to carry and they buckled, giving way to uncontrollable tears that cascaded down my face. This, and many more similar incidents, informed my decision to not accept the proposal of anybody asking for my hand as a second wife at the time. I really wanted to prove her wrong, but I eventually fell prey to a chameleon again!

Another challenge often faced by divorcees within the cultural/emotional context is the fear that they would never heal from the perceived disgrace that often accompanies divorce in many communities. In truth, their fear is not unfounded, as this is often the case in many communities, irrespective of their religious inclination. The more culturally inclined a community is, the more intense the stigma associated with divorce. It is also important to note that these cultural issues are present irrespective of whether your divorce was asked for or you were pushed out. In the event your divorce was sprung on you, the anguish from these cultural and social biases towards divorcees cuts even deeper than the initial setback presented in the marriage. *Laa hawla wa la quwwata illa billaah*.

How did we move from being a lovely support for our sisters to being so judgemental? Why should we let unnecessary cultural conditioning get in our way of being humane? Judgement over support is probably the result of us looking at the world through one lens - our cultural values lens. As beautiful as culture can be, it shouldn't make us cold-hearted; our cultural values shouldn't dictate how we relate to sisters in pain. I believe whenever cultural principles contradict our religious values, we dump these erroneous principles and hold on fast to the religious dictates. Sadly, many do not take to this ideology.

I honestly don't know where the courage to defy all odds and not become a social recluse came from. I guess taking it a day at a time was one of the tools I used to succeed during this phase of my life.

Another challenge faced by divorcees is often encountered at the remarrying phase where they face humongous walls people have erected and labelled 'societal pressures'. These challenges usually stem from the immediate and extended relatives of the might-be husband. You hear statements like "Was she the only girl you saw?"; "Didn't you see young never-married ladies?"; "How can you accept having to raise another man's child?" and so on. This kind of talk further creates a heavy block in the path of recovery for one going through a divorce. Do not give permission to **anyone** to put you down in any way, as a lot of people pass judgement without knowing the facts of what led to the end of a marriage. At such instances, it's paramount to have full certainty that Allaah will look after you. This certainty in your heart will become a source of solace when the skies darken and the clouds drop their load. Hold firm to the belief that Allaah will not desert you as long as you fully trust in Him.

HOW CAN THE ONE GOING THROUGH DIVORCE OVERCOME THESE DEMORALISING ISSUES?

First and foremost, you need to remember that your divorce is a trial from Allaah and it never rains forever, so focus on trying to spot the beauty in the situation and not the enormity of the grey clouds.

My dear sister, if you are struggling to navigate the painful throes of divorce, yet are almost drowning under the weight of cultural stereotypes, do not despair. Allaah is indeed near as He says, "Indeed, the mercy of Allaah is near to the doers of good." [24]

It is also important that you know that the life of this world is filled with all sorts of challenges - some worse than others.

Sometimes when wading through these tests, you'll tell yourself that your situation is the worst. Yet, you only need to raise your head and look around for a few minutes to realise you are indeed one of the most favoured by Allaah (subhaanahu wa ta'ala). Whatever happened in the marriage, however hard you had worked, when there is life, there is hope. And let's assume that indeed your trials are the worst, the fact you are alive and believe in the oneness of God in your heart is sufficient reason to show immense gratitude to Allaah (azza wa jaal).

I remember once when I felt overwhelmed by the immensity of the trials that had hit me; I was in what felt like the deepest pit of darkness and despair. Alhamdulillah, Allaah guided me to a verse of the Qur'an and I immediately gained strength from it. *"Or do you think you that you will enter Paradise while such [trial] has not yet come to you as came to those who passed on before you? They were touched by severe poverty and hardship and were shaken until [even their] messenger and those who believed with him said, "When is the help of Allaah?" Unquestionably, the help of Allaah is near." [25]*

This verse was shown to me by one of my teachers shortly after my divorce. On that particular day, it was obvious to anyone who knew me that something was wrong. The night before, I'd received a horrific text message from the mother of a supposedly close friend prior to divorce. She was someone I looked up to as a mother figure as well, but I guess when the chips are down, 'oju oloju kole dabi oju enii' which means what is not yours cannot feel like yours in the end.

24. Surah al-A'raf: 56
25. Surah al-Baqarah: 214

I gained strength through the aforementioned verse and I sincerely hope it is a source of solace for you. Whenever I became choked-up and couldn't breathe due to the burden of despair gnawing at me, I turned to the words of Allaah and immediately found strength. His words fortify my heart because I know they hold truth I need to hear, and I'm always reassured that if I persevere through the rough patches, my Lord will reward me tenfold.

This certainty in the mercy of my Lord towards His slaves uplifts my spirit and helps me push through whatever challenges I face, irrespective of their magnitude. May you find strength in the words of Allaah. Aamiyn.

In addition to benefitting greatly from reading Allaah's words, another place I found relief was in studying the seerah of the Nabiy (sallAllaahu alayhi wasallam) and his many ahadith. In fact, I sometimes used to be so engrossed in my reading about his (sallAllaahu alayhi wasallam) life, that I would forget all about my challenges. Most times, my trial would seem minor in comparison to what he (sallAllaahu alayhi wasallam) had to go through at the hands of the polytheists and hypocrites. At such times, I immediately become thankful to Allaah, but of course this state didn't last long as humankind was created of a hasty temperament. [26]

One hadith I gained strength from is one in which the Nabiy (sallAllaahu alayhi wasallam) was reported to have said, "The greatest reward comes from the greatest trial. **When Allaah loves a people, He tests them, and whoever accepts it gains the pleasure of Allaah and whoever complains earns His wrath."** [27]

Another one which helped me have patience is one in which the Nabiy (sallAllaahu alayhi wasallam) said, "When Allaah wills good for His slave, He hastens his punishment in this world; and when He wills bad for His slave, He withholds his sins until he comes with them on the Day of Judgement." [28]

Through it all I used to remind myself that good was from Allaah and evil was from what my hands had sent forth and that by the will and permission of Allaah, I would come out of the trial purified and closer to my Rabb. This thought helped me push through the hardest parts of my challenges, especially when 'cultural ideals' crushed me. If you ask me, I think the cultural challenges I endured were greater than the emotional turmoil. Everywhere I looked there was someone willing to malign my

26. Surah al-Maarij 19
27. Sunan at-Tirmidhi, 2396; Ibn Majah, 4031, classed as sahih by Shaykh Al-Albaani (rahimahullaah)
28. Sunan at-Tirmidhi, 2396 classed as sahih by Shaykh Al-Albaani (rahimahullaah)

person; some people who I had hardly ever spoken to up to that point had different tales to narrate, despite barely knowing me.

I remember one day, whilst I was at my madrasah, a sister who I had just recently met came to tell me about what another sister had said to her. I found this bizarre as I wouldn't have been able to recognise the sister who had spoken ill of me to her if I saw her on the street. Yes, I had heard her name before, but not around anyone I knew closely. So to have her dissect my character like she was my family surgeon was surprising to me.

I immediately said to the tale-bearer, "What you have done is tale-bearing and what the sister you sat with has done is slander. Tell her that if she doesn't repent from this, she is trying to bring the wrath of Allaah upon herself!"

My dear sister, know that not a leaf falls except that He (subhaanahu wa ta'ala) knows it. How then can you be in pain without His knowledge? The parable I use when I speak to my dearest ones struggling through this trial or any other trial is, just as gold has to go through the fire to be purified and moulded into appealing shapes, our trials serve as fire or hot coal that helps us become purified for Jannah - our ultimate goal.

Another thing to hold on to when cultural idiosyncrasies creep into the attitude of people towards you following a divorce is that Allaah's promises are true. When He (subhaanahu wa ta'ala) promises, He delivers. Now, which promise am I referring to? The one in the following verse:
"Allaah does not burden a soul except [with that within] its capacity." [29]

Whenever I am going through a rough patch and it feels like I'm crumbling, I remember this verse and immediately look inwards. I usually feel strengthened, as it helps calm my heart so I can put my trust in Him. I take consolation in the fact that the trial is not bigger than the strength Allaah has blessed me with, and if I look inwards, I will find all the tools I need to excel.

Lastly, please do not allow unfounded cultural ideologies to ruin your standing with Allaah (subhaanahu wa ta'ala). There are many times people hold on to marriages where they and their partner are working towards earning the displeasure of Allaah (subhaanahu wa ta'ala). Instead of emptying their dirt-filled hands and filling them with good, they stick their neck right in because they fear the societal pressure,

---

29. Surah al-Baqarah: 286

despite Allaah (subhaanahu wa ta'ala) being the One to be most mindful of.

My dear one, whenever you focus on doing an act sincerely for the sake of Allaah, He will fill it with fulfilment and goodness. Even when you face challenges upon that path, He (subhaanahu wa ta'ala) grants you the tawfeeq to get through it and come out better than before you entered.

You just need to trust in Allaah and work hard at sustaining a relationship with your Rabb, for He is indeed the Best of those who guide. It is He alone who can protect you and He will suffice you should you decide to stand up against the cultural pressures when going through a divorce. And Allaah is sufficient for those who put their trust in Him.

"You shall surely be tested in your possessions and in yourselves. And you will surely hear from those who were given the scripture before you and from those who associate others with Allaah much abuse. But if you are patient and fear Allaah - indeed, that is of the matters [worthy] of determination."[30]

POINTS TO PONDER:

Allaah alone is our Lord and Sustainer, and only He sets the rules for what should or shouldn't be. Do not let anyone put you down or label you, as is often the case following a divorce.

Please do not allow cultural pressure to push you to doing something you probably wouldn't have normally done, such as jumping into another marriage with the first person that approaches you with a set of white teeth.

Make the words of Allaah and ahadith of His Nabiy (sallAllaahu alayhi wasallam) your friends at times of trials.

Most importantly, when it seems like everyone has forsaken you due to one preconceived idea of what the ideal is, know that Allaah (subhaanahu wa ta'ala) is always near. He knows your every pain and He has the answers to all your problems - big and small.

---

30. Surah al Imran: 186

CHAPTER 3
COPING WITH THE AFTERMATH OF DIVORCE

"And the Hereafter is better for you than the first [life]." [31]

I remember once listening to the tafsir of the above verse of the Qur'an during the period following my *'iddah*. It was when I was still unstable and battling my demons that I listened to the teacher explain how the Nabiy (sallAllaahu alayhi wasallam) had been through a lot of hardship, and the aforementioned verse was a consolation for him. I immediately burst into tears and I was quite inconsolable for some time, but then I listened to the tafsir again and I saw the beauty behind the verse.

One of the things that made the aftermath of my divorce painful was the fact that I realised I was living in a fool's paradise when I had to face my trials. The crowd around me thinned out to the point that I almost needed binoculars to be able to see the ones that stayed put! *Alhamdulilaah*, I had those who stayed and didn't desert me, yet I know others aren't that fortunate. The moment they fall into a trial of this magnitude, everyone immediately disappears, leaving them bereft of a stronghold or even the thinnest shoulder to rest on. I've come to realise that you don't actually lose friends, you lose the shafts you assumed were grains amongst the crowd around you. Don't lose any sleep over them, the ones who stick around during a trial are the real deal.

Being divorced has a lot of associated challenges, some of which can be lifelong if you allow people's opinions to dictate the way you live your life. The magnitude of the aftermath varies from person to person. Some handle it with courage, damn all consequences and stand firm, completely unperturbed by the bickering of the people around them. This group of people are *very* few. Most people find it hard to separate themselves from the noise people make and the cultural baggage they bring, to dictate who is successful and who is not.

I do think that the length of time is not an indicator of how successful a marriage is. There is no clear-cut definition of a successful marriage, as different people have their individual wants and needs in their union.

---

31. Surah ad-Duha, 1

According to Glennon Doyle Melton, "A marriage is not only a success if it lasts forever, but if it changes both partners into more loving, free, wise, brave, kind, whole beings."

I once met a couple of almost 30 years, and despite the longevity of their relationship, there was still a huge gap between them. When I asked the wife about it, she had so much to say. She was, in fact, heartbroken and had resigned herself to a life of unfulfilled marital desires.

IS HELP AVAILABLE?

In my own experience, I barely saw external help available. There was no support group or system in place to help the transition in any way. In fact, the direct opposite was the case. Instead of support, I saw more people working hard at dragging my name in the mud and working to ensure that I wasn't able to resurface back into the community. Unfortunately for them, I was tougher than I looked and more importantly, I had faith in the One who is the best Disposer of Affairs, Al-Wakeel! *Alhamdulilaah*.

For many going through divorce, this is their reality. It's almost like a competition of who is going to say the worst about who. As if the ongoing war with the ex isn't bad enough, some people start carrying tales about their least favourite person amongst the estranged couple in the name of intending to reconcile the couple. It is sad they do not reflect on their actions, realising that whatever they say goes right into their book of deeds.

I must be honest, I almost got into the same blame game I mentioned earlier when I went through divorce, but then I got some advice from my sister and that advice served me well. She called me a few months into the whole saga - we were living in different countries at the time, so she didn't have quick access to me following my divorce.

She said to me, "My dear sister, I know it must be really tough for you right now. I haven't been through what you're going through at the moment, so I might not have the best piece of advice for you and I pray Allaah saves me from it, but I think it's about time you went along the path of your role model 'Aaishah (radiyAllaahu anha). Just like she kept quiet when she was accused during the issue of her slander, you are also going to keep quiet and say nothing to anyone. And Allaah will vindicate you by granting you *tawfeeq* in a way that would put your heart at rest, just as He (subhaanahu wa ta'ala) exonerated 'Aaishah (radiyAllaahu anha)." She went on to say,

"It doesn't matter if you do not get help here. Have *yaqeen* that whatever you send forth will not go unnoticed by the One who witnesses all things."

On hearing that, I thought, 'How can she say that? Does she even know what my ex has been saying about me?' It was almost like she'd heard my thoughts because her next statements were, "No matter how much he talks, you must strive to be the bigger person and keep quiet. If he refuses to act differently, you shouldn't follow his footsteps."

Then she asked, "If a mentally ill person threw a stone at you whilst you were walking peacefully on the road, would you throw a stone back at the person or run after him? Just like you wouldn't do that, why not employ that same tactic when relating with people who come to you about what your ex-husband is saying?"

Again, this was one of the best pieces of advice I got at that time and it reminds me of the saying of Ali ibn Abi Taalib (radiyAllaahu anhu): "Be like the flower that gives its fragrance to even the hand that crushes it." I found a lot of peace acting upon my sister's counsel. It wasn't easy at first, but I eventually worked harder at being silent in the face of people's talk, that in no time, I had perfected the art of going mute. *Alhamdulilaah*, Allaah has given me the blessing of being this way ever since.

WHY DO I SHARE THIS WITH YOU?

Just like I learnt to the art of being silent, you can learn to sharpen this skill as well. One of the things that aided my becoming upright upon this stance was the realisation that a lot of people would come to meet me just because they want to hear what happened, not because they really intend to make a difference or resolve the problems I had. So wouldn't it be better if one just remained silent, directing one's pain and grief to the One that can soothe your heart and grant you relief?

"Unquestionably, by the remembrance of Allaah, hearts are assured." [32]

So, in order to aid your silence, immerse yourself in the remembrance of Allaah. Verily, your heart will find rest when you are sincerely seeking His pleasure through constant remembrance of Him. Allaah's support is the most beneficial support you can ever have. His support is available anytime you need it; all you need to do is turn to Him and He is ever-ready to forgive, purify, and guide you through the pain.

---

32. Surah ar-Ra'd: 28

You might be thinking, *it's easier said than done*, and I agree completely. I had some pretty rough days where I would read verses from the Qur'an and cry to my heart's fill. This release was necessary to aid the healing process, and I'm grateful for the solitude in which to shed those tears, all the while knowing that only Allaah could bring me out of the darkness enveloping me into the light of tranquillity and contentment.

FINDING SOLACE IN SILENCE AND PRAYER

Alhamdulilaah, there are now lots of resources online for anyone going through divorce. Just to mention a few:

I run a support group - Siddiqah - which is currently based in Nigeria, but plans to spread their work to other countries in the not-too-distant future, In Shaa Allaah. You can follow Siddiqah's work as well as their motivational short quotes via their Facebook page at: www.facebook.com/siddiqahcic, or check out their website at: www.siddiqah.org.

There is also Continuum, as well as My Iddah, which has an online base at: www.my-iddah.com. My Iddah has a lot of resources to soothe the hearts of those going through this trying time.

SEEK HELP FROM TRUSTED SOURCES

Some are able to rise quickly after a disaster, others crawl out from the debris, while others unfortunately remain lying on the ground. In the event that the latter receive support to get up, they do so graciously to the delight of all and sundry. I didn't have the strongest circle of support, but *Alhamdulilaah*, I pulled through. There are those who aren't so fortunate, hence why I set up a support group for women going through the throes of divorce and *'iddah*.

If you need help getting through the psychological and emotional distress that usually accompanies divorce, please do not shy away from speaking about it, even if certain people chastise you for doing so due to their lack of knowledge. Let off steam in the best way possible and reach out to someone whom you know might be able to serve as a pillar of strength for you, and don't hold back from crying to Allaah.

Once, I was almost choking from the truth of betrayal following my divorce when I got a call from my sister. Her timing couldn't have been better! The words she shared with me that day brought both relief and an emotional flood, but they helped me think a bit more rationally and pull myself up. She said to me, "Do you know you are a very strong person?" I remained silent so she continued, "You have been through things in the past that has proven to us that you are indeed strong. Please find that strength again and push through these stormy clouds."

That was the push that caused the clouds to part as I cried my eyes out. She stayed with me on the phone until I calmed down, then dropped me some messages afterwards.

Although my support system during my *'iddah* and the period following it might not have been the strongest, I wasn't completely without support. If for some reason you lack a solid pillar to stay upright, as is the case with many people, reach out to organisations like Siddiqah or Continuum as they have a system in place to help people going through divorce, including online resources as well as dedicated personnel to assist you. Do not despair or lose hope, for verily Allaah is with you.

POINTS TO PONDER:
The strongest support you could ever have is Allaah - turn to Him and you will be at peace.

If you are in need of resources to help you pull through *'iddah*, you can get online resources at: www.my-iddah.com. You could also drop a message for Siddiqah via their email address at siddiqah.cic@gmail.com for more personalised support.

You could also speak to someone trusted around you who you know is sincere and truthful.

Ultimately, the only One who can bring us out from every hardship in the life of this world is Allaah. We cannot run away from challenges. In fact, our being on earth is in and of itself a trial. As such, it is incumbent that we develop coping mechanisms to help us get through the rough patches we may experience. Hold on to Him through good and bad times and you will never go wrong.

"The reality is that the only way to truly come through the grieving process is to sit with the pain and recognise it for what it is: the way in which Allaah created us to cope with extreme loss. That is why 'iddah is a gift from Allaah, not a form of punishment." - Kaighla Um Dayo, My Iddah

And in the end, all praise and adoration are due to Allaah alone, Lord of the worlds.

EPILOGUE

"If you are grateful, I will surely increase you [in favour];
but if you deny, indeed, My punishment is severe."
-Surah Ibrahim: 7

TELLING IT AS IT IS:
REAL STORIES FROM WOMEN

Although permissible, in recent years, the divorce statistics have reached epidemic proportions and there are multitudes of reasons why marriages are ending. Common reasons are incompatibility - especially due to religious conflicts, and abuse - either physical or emotional, although divorce is not limited to just these reasons. While some couples fall out of love or grow apart, other marriages dissolve as a result of infidelity, leaving some women feeling they need to leave the marriage altogether. Regardless of the reasons for a marriage ending, it takes time to bounce back, and for some this may be a tough road to happiness - especially with the stigmatisation from a society where people make unfair assumptions about those who get divorced.

Below are interviews of sisters at different places in their post-marriage journeys. For some it has been wonderful, for others not so much. Perhaps you might be able to learn one or two things from their experiences.

INTERVIEW 1
Name: Umm Jamal
Age: 39 years

AA: As salamu alaykum wa rahmatullaah wa barakatuhu
UJ: Wa alaykumusalam wa rahmatullaah wa barakatuhu

AA: Can you please give us a brief background of what your marriage was like: how long you were married for, whether you would you say you were deeply in love during the marriage and whether you have children?
UJ: I was married for 2 years and 10 months. No, I was not in love at all. I married him because I believed it was the right thing to do, since he appeared to have a good character. I believed true love would come after marriage, so I was prepared to work at nurturing the love afterwards. We didn't have any children as I suffered a number of miscarriages.

AA: How long was your courtship before the eventual marriage? Do you think the length of the courtship had anything to do with the divorce?

UJ: We didn't exactly court since courtship as it's done in our times is not allowed in Islam. We knew each other for a few months before we got married. I do not think the length of courtship had anything to do with the divorce; I have seen people who courted for 7 years get married and still get divorced after about 5 years.

AA: Did you notice any red flags before marriage? Red flags are actions and ideas that do not really settle well with you, but you feel you can cope with when married or you hope will change.

UJ: Oh yes, there were red flags. At the time, I didn't realise they were red flags, though. I just told myself he was probably tense and excited by the whole marriage thing. I only had myself to blame for turning a blind eye to the warning signs.

AA: Was the divorce initiated by your husband or did you request it? What was the deal breaker that made you give it all up and decide to walk away? How did you cope during the 'iddah period?

UJ: I asked for the divorce. Well, deal breaker? I had been going through a lot of distress. Many times I was sad almost to the point of depression, but I used to mask it with silly jokes and unnecessary laughter on topics that were not funny. I guess I eventually owned up to myself that the marriage wasn't working and it was best if I left, but I was worried I didn't have anything serious to use as a valid reason, even though he had previously assaulted me. Perhaps an answer to my du'a came in the form of a major assault. It was so huge that I immediately said, "I'm not taking this anymore. I think this is my cue to leave."

Coping with the *'iddah* was a different ball game. I was in a place where there was barely any support of any kind. I didn't want anyone looking down at me, so I initially kept the information of my divorce to myself and told only those whom I considered to be very close. Eventually, I decided to hold my head up high and somewhere along the line I grew a thick skin to all the judgemental attitude being thrown my way. *Alhamdulilaah*, Allaah strengthened me and I eventually pulled through.

AA: Prior to your separation, were there efforts to resolve the issues, and was there any involvement of relatives and maybe community elders? Did you seek help via professional or spiritual counselling to salvage the marriage?

UJ: Well, there was no effort at resolving issues until after issues had gotten to a head with us. We still ventured near counselling, but it wasn't able to help work us through, as a lot of water had already gone under the bridge.

AA: How did your family and friends handle your decision? Were you open enough to disclose any emotional and psychological pain you may have felt?
UJ: As for my family, it was sort of hard for them. A lot of the things they got to hear about after the divorce, they hadn't heard about prior to that time. They didn't understand why I had kept quiet for that long. In my defence, I'd say, I was actually telling them indirectly - they just didn't understand what I was saying!

I didn't discuss the pain I was going through because I perceived an attitude of them wanting me to suck up the pain and be macho. I didn't think I was going to be able to do that so I only turned to them whenever the pressure got too much for me.

AA: Were you working / earning an income? How have you been able to cope without spousal support?
UJ: During the marriage, finances were very tight. There were many times I had to learn to go without, so when it ended I just sort of switched back to my hibernation mode. Fortunately for me though, I had just gotten a job a few months before the incident that led to the divorce, so becoming stable was my focus when I realised I was going to have to be on my own. To achieve some level of stability, I had to get a second job just to make ends meet.

AA: Do you feel stigmatised by the label 'divorcee'?
UJ: Sometimes I do, sometimes I can't be bothered.

AA: How easy has it been moving on? Have you remarried or have you ever considered it? How true is the myth that only divorcees, widowers, and polygamists are the only options for divorcees in rebuilding their lives?
UJ: *Alhamdulilaah*, I am remarried now and settled. At first, it wasn't easy moving on. I wasn't ready to commit to another man that looked good, only to discover he was same as before. But Allaah does what He wills and He is in control of our hearts.

No, I disagree with that myth. There are loads of cases in which divorcees have been known to marry single guys, it all depends on your preference. Some of us come out of the divorce period with the intention of moving on only with someone who has a proven track record of treating women well, which implies that there has to be a woman or family one can ask.

AA: Were your family and friends accommodating enough to provide support for you through the process? Were there support groups available to assist you with closure and discussing your next plans?

UJ: My family tried to provide support in the way they knew best, but it was sometimes perceived as undue pressure. Sometimes, all one needs is someone to just squeeze your hands and remind you it'll soon pass over. No, there were no support groups anywhere. At least none in the Muslim community I was affiliated with at the time.

AA: *Do you think the Muslim community reacts well or provides adequate support to divorcees?*
UJ: Sadly, the Muslim community does **not** respond well to the plight of divorcees. In fact, they are more segregated and ostracised in the Muslim community than in any other.

AA: *What advice do you have for women contemplating divorce and women who are divorced, but are still unable to grasp the reality?*
UJ: Have loads of patience whilst you still can. In the event you fear for your life or sanity of mind, perhaps a divorce is better than waiting to see what would happen next. In the event you worked really hard and still got divorced, take consolation in the fact that Allaah is Al-Hakeem, the Wise; your divorce has happened for a reason and if you're patient, the lessons in your trial will become apparent and a means of goodness for you.

AA: *If you know of any support group for divorced women, will you be willing participate actively, share your experience, and provide support for other women?*
UJ: Yes, I will! I am all for lending help to people going through difficulties in life.

INTERVIEW 2
Name: Umm Faatimah
Age: 25 years

AA: *As salamu alaykum wa rahmatullaah wa barakatuhu*
UF: Wa alaykumusalam wa rahmatullaah wa barakatuhu

AA: *Can you please give us a brief background of what your marriage was like: how long you were married for, whether you would you say you were deeply in love during the marriage and whether you have children?*
UF: I was married for about 4 years, from 2010 to around March/April 2014. I would say I really liked him, hence I accepted his proposal. The attraction at the time was what appeared to me as attachment to the deen. Yes, we had a child together.

AA: How long was your courtship before the eventual marriage? Do you think the length of the courtship had anything to do with the divorce?

UF: Since courtship in the real sense is not allowed in Islam, I won't say we 'courted'. What we had was the period between meeting and having our nikah. That wasn't very long. Irrespective of how long we knew ourselves before marriage, I don't think long courtship would have helped us know each other better. You don't know a man until you start living with him day in, day out.

AA: Did you notice any red flags before marriage?

UF: No, I didn't notice red flags. They were probably there without me paying much attention to them, especially as I was very young and excited about the prospect of getting married. One thing I should definitely not have agreed to though, was living with his parents. It caused more problems than I ever imagined.

AA: Was the divorce initiated by your husband or did you request it? How did you cope during the 'iddah period?

UF: The divorce was initiated by him. I was in shock for the better part, as I didn't understand how the marriage could have ended that abruptly. He just came to say he didn't think we were compatible and we'd need to go our separate ways - after 4 years! Now, you don't think we're compatible? It sounded absurd to me, but I couldn't do anything to stop it as all my pleas fell on deaf ears. It seemed like he had made up his mind.

AA: Prior to your separation, were there efforts to resolve the issues, and was there any involvement of relatives and maybe community elders? Did you seek help via professional or spiritual counselling to salvage the marriage?

UF: We never saw a counsellor. I didn't even realise the problems were that serious. We weren't even having fights that frequently. I did notice him having constant discussions with his parents at the time, as we were living with them, and each time he came out from those discussions his countenance usually wasn't very good. All efforts to find out what happened between him and his parents were always futile. I tried to get us to see a spiritual counsellor, but all efforts towards achieving that failed.

AA: How did your family and friends handle your decision? Were you open enough to disclose any emotional and psychological pain you may have felt?

UF: The divorce wasn't my decision, so we were all forced to accept it as much as we hated it. I haven't quite got over the emotional and psychological pain of my experience. There are good days and bad days. I only recently found a support group that has been of great help.

AA: Was child custody and access an issue? If so, what principles were considered in determining custody and access? How did you minimise the effect of the divorce on the children, and how did you break the separation to them?

UF: Though we had a child, custody wasn't decided the legitimate way as I just had my daughter taken off me the day I was asked to pack out. I didn't even get to complete my *'iddah* under the same roof as him. It was almost like his parents were intent on the marriage ending. I rarely get to see my daughter, so I'm unable to cushion the effects of the divorce on her.

AA: Were you working /earning an income? How have you been able to cope without spousal support?

UF: No, I wasn't. I was still in school when the divorce happened. It has been a bit tough being out there on my own, but all praise is still due to Allaah.

AA: Do you feel stigmatised by the label 'divorcee'?

UF: Yes, I feel stigmatised. I get poor treatment from supposed friends and you can only imagine how non-friends treat me.

AA: How easy has it been moving on? Have you remarried or have you ever considered it?

UF: It's been two years since my divorce, yet I've been unable to move on because there's been no closure for the matter. I need to heal before I can start to contemplate remarrying. There was one attempt to move on, but it ended badly, so I decided to take things easy.

AA: Were your family and friends accommodating enough to provide support for you through the process? Were there support groups available to assist you with closure and discussing your next plans?

UF: My family have tried to the best of their ability. As for friends, some have disappeared, others have started giving me an attitude, and some others have remained true. *Alhamdulilaah.*

When I was struggling through it, I heard of Siddiqah. The sister in charge of Siddiqah met with me to discuss what happened, and she has been very helpful and supportive.

AA: Do you think the Muslim community reacts well or provides support to divorcees?

UF: I don't think the Muslim community reacts well to the plight of divorcees. It takes immense efforts on your part before you can mingle and attend programs or Muslim gatherings. Some people treat you as though you are infectious. Some others start to hide their husbands from you, perhaps out of fear of you becoming a wife as well.

AA: What advice do you have for women contemplating divorce and women who are divorced, but are still unable to grasp the reality?
UF: If you're going through divorce, have patience and everything will come in its own time. Patience is key.

AA: If you know of any support group for divorced women, will you be willing participate actively, share your experience, and provide support for other women?
UF: Yes, I will. I'm not in the best place to help someone now though, as I'm still unstable; but I'd be happy to help someone else.

AA: Ukhtii, Jazaakumullaahu khayran for your time. This interview has been insightful. On a personal note, though, can I ask, do you miss your ex-husband? Do you feel you could have done some things differently, and if asked back would you re-marry him?
UF: Yes, I miss my ex-husband. I would be happy for a reconciliation, especially since I wasn't the one who sought to leave. Even though I didn't ask for the divorce, perhaps I could have sought help earlier.

When I think back now, there were one or two challenges we had where perhaps I could have acted differently. In my defence, I was trying to work on him improving without realising it was only creating a wedge between us. And I definitely shouldn't have agreed to live with my in-laws as it put a lot of strain on our marriage.

INTERVIEW 3
Name: Umm Bilal
Age: 29

AA: As salamu alaykum wa rahmatullaah wa barakatuhu
UB: Wa alaykumusalam wa rahmatullaah wa barakatuhu

AA: Can you please give us a brief background of what your marriage has been like and how long you've been married for? Would you say you are deeply in love? Do you have children?
UB: *Alhamdulilaah*, I have been married for 6 years now, and yes I would say I am truly in love with my husband and happy in my marriage. Allaah has blessed us with 2

boys and we are all happy and content with His favours.

AA: How long was your courtship before the eventual marriage? Do you think the length of the courtship has anything to do with the turn out of your marriage?
UB: We courted for around two years, not because we wanted to wait that long, but my father was very old-school. He believed my older siblings had to get married before I did. Needless to say, it took a lot of family meetings and pleading to get him to allow the wedding.

However, looking back I am happy I was forced to wait that long because in the course of the two years, I became more mature and more aware of what I wanted out of marriage. I came to understand my intended and had struck a very cordial relationship with my in-laws, so there were no unwanted surprises.

AA: How did you decide he was 'the one'?
UB: Well, he is no 'tall, dark and handsome'! I was not instantly attracted to him at first, partly because I was well sought-after and I had a sea of options. During that period, I was about to accept the proposal of someone else and was working up the courage to tell my parents, but then I lost my mother, and I suddenly learnt to grow up fast. You see, I always had the ideology that I could change a man to be 'the man'. This guy was a chain smoker and he told me, "Baby, for you I will stop." SubhanAllaah, if his mother or his love for Allaah couldn't get him to stop, then what was so special about me? I came to my senses fast. Then of course, there was the *efiko* guy that would jump if I told him to - he would literally do anything I asked him. Initially, it was cute to have a guy give an arm and a leg for you, but I wasn't looking for a docile man that followed me around, who had no initiative of his own. My friends constantly teased that I had put a love potion in his vegetable soup - *haha!*

Alhamdulilaah for the plethora of choices. There was something about my husband that stood out. He is much older than I am, but we clicked on so many levels, we have similar interests and till today we are still always giddy and chatty.

AA: How is your marriage?
UB: Honestly, I believe a woman holds all the aces (at least most of them). I learn to pick my battles. I am not forceful, neither am I docile, so I would say there's a fine balance. Even though he is much older than I am, we talk like friends. We communicate a lot about things as mundane as how many times I went to toilet to things as serious as how we want to invest our money. We have sex talks too when we feel like there are dry spells coming up or if we need to ignite our spark again. Nothing is off limits with

us. We have our date nights, when we drop the children off with family just so we can rediscover ourselves - because in the hustle of being a working parent, there are times when we totally neglect ourselves sexually. All in all, I think I am having a ball. *Alhamdulilaah.*

AA: Do you have fights or quarrel?
UB: Of course, we do. Once, at the beginning of our marriage, on my way back from work I went to the market, came back home and immediately went to the kitchen to cook what I thought was the most delicious bowl of *efo riro*[33] soup. Without warning, he simply told me that he had eaten a heavy lunch and wasn't hungry. *Ahhhh!* I sat him down and force-fed him like a baby. From then on, I learnt that a simple, *Honey are you hungry?* can save me from flaring up. The key for me is, I have learnt to understand my husband and I know what battles I can't win. I am quick to say sorry and kneel down and beg when the need arises. But then there are times when he is at fault and I make him beg. Like I said, we have the aces; it's all about knowing how to play the cards right.

AA: What is your relationship like with your in-laws?
UB: I don't interfere with his relationship with his family. It's not my business how much money he wants to spend on his mum or if he wants to buy a pair of new shoes for his dad. In fact, I encourage him to do more because as we all know, in our culture, if the husband misbehaves, the wife gets all the blame. I never go to visit empty-handed and it's safe to say I am the favourite daughter-in-law (my brother-in-law's wife is constantly surprised when my mother-in-law calls me up to have a chat before anyone else). So I would say yes, I have a good relationship with them. In fact, my sister-in-law always asks me for my secret.

AA: What advice do you have for women choosing a spouse?
UB: Marrying your best friend is important. When all the butterflies settle and your clothes size changes from a size 8 to a size 16, your friendship with your husband will always keep the marriage alive. Allow him to retain his personality. Not all men like it when they are with their boys and hear remarks about how they have changed - they still want to retain some semblance of themselves and may start to resent you for forcing a certain persona onto them. Treat them with love and respect and always pray with and for them.
Personally, I never allow a third party into my home matters. No matter how bad a dispute, we resolve it among ourselves. The lesser your family tales become talk on somebody else's dinner table, the longer-lasting your marriage will be. And even

---

33. A spicy Nigerian spinach stew

more importantly, I try to look appealing and sexy for my husband. I work out at least 3 times a week - after two kids my body isn't as it was six years ago. I reserve my traditional dresses for parties and rock all my skinny jeans and tank tops in the house. My rule is, 'I wear my hijab so that other men don't lust after me, but when I am at home, I am a vixen'.

INTERVIEW 4
Name: Umm Uthman
Age: 51

AA: As salamu alaykum wa rahmatullaah wa barakatuhu
UU: Wa alaykumusalam wa rahmatullaah wa barakatuhu

AA: Can you please give us a brief background of what your marriage has been like and how long have you been married for? Would you say you are deeply in love? Do you have children?
UU: *Alhamdulilaah*, I have been married for 29 years. Yes! I am deeply in love with my husband with all my heart and happy in my marriage. Allaah has blessed us with six children and we are all happy and content with His favours. I wouldn't say there haven't been challenges, but I'm grateful we've been overcoming them.

AA: How long was your courtship before the eventual marriage? Do you think the length of the courtship has anything to do with the turn out of your marriage?
UU: I met my husband for the first time six years before we eventually married. We met through our parents. His parents and mine didn't live too far apart. In those days, families liked to mingle and they introduced us to each other, but I had to travel to a different city to learn a trade. This caused the delay, as I didn't want to feel like a liability to my husband when we eventually got married. I wanted to be a productive wife, so I decided to equip myself with the necessary skills.

Alhamdulilaah, we got married when I finished. Living in different cities during the period of my apprenticeship further strengthened the decision to wait until I was done before we married. I don't think other people should take this long, though. I would do things differently if I knew what I know now.

That said, I don't think people should marry without a plan. I believe it's important that you plan and work towards your goals. It's important that you have something productive that serves as a cash base for you so your husband doesn't treat you like you are a liability, as is often the case with women I saw who were totally dependent on their husbands.

AA: How did you decide he was 'the one'?
UU: My husband is a fine man, I'm not going to lie about that, but that wasn't why I married him. I recognised a long time ago that beauty and wealth were ephemeral things, so I paid attention to his character. The few times I saw him when I went to visit home, I took time to study his character. I think it's important that more young girls learn to be patient and aren't hasty when they are in the process of making this crucial decision.

It's also important that they communicate their life goals to their intended spouse. I told him my plans and said I wasn't ready to get married when we initially met. He said he understood my stance and didn't push it. Little did I know that he still intended to wait for me.

Alhamdulilaah, I can confidently say I'm a patient person. Plus, I was often busy with my apprenticeship amongst other things I was involved in, so I was able to wait. I don't think anyone should marry based on beauty, though. It's the character that brings out true beauty. His character attracted me. My husband is patient, caring, truthful, and hardworking. These were traits I observed even before we got married and he didn't change when we married. These traits have stayed, and have even improved. I realised we have similarities and so I married him.

AA: How is your marriage?
UU: Our marriage has been nice, *Alhamdulilaah*. But when children are involved, the game changes. The pressure is enormous. Marriage is expected to have its highs and lows anyway. I discuss everything with my husband, every topic under the sun. I'm not afraid to raise an issue with him as I've come to understand him. I try not to make hasty decisions irrespective of the circumstances, I ensure I always carry him along. I try to avoid doing anything we haven't both agreed on and he reciprocates that love and respect as well. It is important for wives to strive to honour and respect their husbands, especially when the children are around, as they are learning from what you do.

AA: Do you have fights or quarrel?
UU: It's impossible for couples not to fight. In fact, it is impossible for two people to live together without disagreeing on one thing or the other. What makes one

marriage different from the other is how the couple choose to solve their differences. We solve our issues amongst ourselves. We don't involve third parties.

If I *must* report him, I look for someone close to him in his family to speak to about it. Someone who can advise him correctly.

I advise couples to strive to not spread tales about their marital woes - find a way to communicate your issues and resolve them amicably. In the event that your husband is very difficult, try to get someone he respects involved, preferably someone from his family.

AA: What is your relationship like with your in-laws?
UU: I don't have problems with them and there wasn't much trouble in the past. I try to maintain a cordial relationship with them. It's been by the help and mercy of Allaah, and my husband helped me by often advising me on how to be with them. He made sure he explained each person's character traits, which helped me work on my relationship with them.

AA: What advice do you have for women choosing a spouse?
UU: Have patience and pay attention to those who ask for your hand in marriage. Try to ensure that the one you agree to is reliable. Watch him carefully - within the confines of the deen, of course. Find out about his means of sustenance, his relationship with his family and siblings, and most importantly, his family history.

Check and be sure that he is caring and responsible. Let him be someone with traceable roots.

A FINAL PIECE OF ADVICE

Sometimes you feel like giving up, probably because it doesn't feel as though things are improving in your marriage or in your life in entirety. It feels like all the troubles of your heart are becoming worse with each new day. You wonder why everything bad is happening to you. You constantly ask yourself, *why me?* You keeping asking from Allaah (subhaanahu wa ta'ala) and often wonder why you're not as fortunate as other people around you. Understand that everybody has their own different life story. Don't compare your own beginning to another person's happy-ever-after ending. You don't know what they have had to go through to arrive at where they currently are. At such times it feels like your supplications are not being accepted. In fact it may feel as though you have been cursed.

But guess what? Allaah (subhaanahu wa ta'ala) might be silent but He watches you day and night. He is All-Knowing, All-Aware. He listens to your supplications and He has something special in stock for you. Stay focused, be strong and hardworking and most importantly, do not stop calling on Him. Know that you're not alone in that hard situation, we are all in this boat together. Please do not give up, your time is coming sooner than you realise.

37324262R10052

Made in the USA
Middletown, DE
27 November 2016